Knots, Bends, and Hitches for Mariners

Knots, Bends, and Hitches for Mariners

The United States Power Squadrons

  INTERNATIONAL MARINE / McGRAW-HILL
Camden, Maine ◦ New York ◦ Chicago ◦ San Francisco ◦ Lisbon
London ◦ Madrid ◦ Mexico City ◦ Milan ◦ New Delhi
San Juan ◦ Seoul ◦ Singapore ◦ Sydney ◦ Toronto

The McGraw·Hill Companies

1 2 3 4 5 6 7 8 9 DOC DOC 9 8 7 6 5
© 2006 by United States Power Squadrons

All rights reserved. The publisher takes no responsibility for the use of any of the materials or methods described in this book, nor for the products thereof. The name "International Marine" and the International Marine logo are trademarks of The McGraw-Hill Companies. Printed in the United States of America.

Library of Congress Cataloging-in-Publication Data
Knots, bends, and hitches for mariners / the United States Power Squadrons.
   p.   cm.
Includes bibliographical references and index.
  ISBN 0-07-146321-6 (spiral bound : alk. paper)
  1. Knots and splices. I. United States Power Squadrons.
VM533.K65 2006
623.88'82—dc22   2005026413

Questions regarding the content of this book should be addressed to
International Marine
P.O. Box 220
Camden, ME 04848
www.internationalmarine.com

Questions regarding the ordering of this book should be addressed to
The McGraw-Hill Companies
Customer Service Department
P.O. Box 547
Blacklick, OH 43004
Retail customers: 1-800-262-4729
Bookstores: 1-800-722-4726

Illustrations by Madison Avenue West and Irene Rodriguez.
Chapter opener photo of a Bowline by Corinne J. Humphrey/IndexStock.

Contents

Acknowledgments	viii
① Marlinespike Seamanship: An Introduction	1
② Marlinespike Seamanship Terminology	3

Parts of a Line — 3
Basic Rope Configurations — 4
    Bight — 4
    Turn — 5
    Jam Turn — 5
    Round Turn — 7
    Overhand Loop — 7
    Underhand Loop — 7
    Half Hitch — 8
Breaking Strength Versus Working Strength — 8
Knots Weaken Rope — 9
Knots, Bends, Hitches, and Splices — 9

③ Working with Rope — 11

Rope Materials — 11
Rope Construction — 13
    Laid Rope — 13
    Single-Braid Rope — 14
    Double-Braid Rope — 14
    Parallel-Core Rope — 15
Common Rope Uses Aboard — 16
Cutting Rope — 17
    Cold Cutting — 17
    Heat Cutting — 17
Joining Rope — 19
    Using Heat — 19
    Using Glue — 19
Dyeing Rope — 20
    Equipment for Dyeing Rope — 20
    Dyeing Method — 21

Contents

Line Ends (Whipping Lines)	22
Seizing Lines	24
Care of Line	25
Proper Line Storage	29
Marlinespike Seamanship Tools	30

4 Knots 37

Rope Ends (Stopper Knots)	37
Overhand Knot	37
Slipped Overhand Knot (Slip Knot)	37
Figure-Eight Knot	38
Stevedore Knot	38
Blood Knot	41
Heaving Line Knot	42
Monkey's Fist	44
Loop Knots	46
Bowline	46
Bowline on a Bight	46
Slipped Bowline	50
Angler's Loop (Perfection Knot)	50
Painter's Bowline	50
Spanish Bowline	55
Japanese Bowline	57
Three-Part Crown Knot	59
True Lover's Knot (Clover Knot or Cross Knot)	61
Japanese Success Knot	63
Jury Mast Knot	65

5 Bends 68

Sheet Bend	68
Double Sheet Bend	70
Becket Bend (Becket Hitch)	70
Carrick Bend	72
Hawser Bend	74
Reef (Square) Knot	76

6 Hitches 78

Attaching Hitches	78
Round Turn with Two Half Hitches	78
Clove Hitch (for tall piles)	80
Clove Hitch (for short piles)	82
Cleat Hitch	82
Anchor Bend (a Hitch)	82
Rolling Hitch	86
Buntline Hitch	88

Contents

Slipped Buntline Hitch	88
Tugboat Hitch (Bitt Hitch)	91
Lark's Head (Cow Hitch)	92
Inside Cow Hitch	93
Jar Sling	95
Gathering Hitches	97
Binder's Loop	97
Sack Knot (Twice-Turned)	98
Sack Knot (Thrice-Turned)	98
Strangle Knot	98
Constrictor Knot	100

Splices 104

Rope Ends	104
Back Splice	105
Wall and Crown Knot	105
Matthew Walker Knot	110
Connecting Ropes	112
Short Splice	113
Long Splice	114
Spliced Eyes	116
Eye Splice (Laid Rope)	116
Eye Splice (Double-Braid Rope)	118
Eye Splice in the Middle of Laid Line	122

Decorative Knots 126

Line Ends	126
Turk's Head	126
Crown Sennit	130
Casting the Crown Sennit	130
Tack Knot	130
Star Knot	132
Bell Rope Sennit	140
Creating the Bell Rope Sennit	141
Cockscombing	143
Toggle Knots	145
Toggled Reef Knot	145
Toggled Lark's Head	145
Toggle and Becket	148

Bibliography 150

Glossary 151

Index 154

Acknowledgments

Many thanks to P/D/C Kenneth N. Beckman, SN; P/D/C John C. Bennett, SN; P/D/C William F. Mullin, AP; Madison Avenue West (illustrations); and D/Lt/C Irene Rodriguez, SN (illustrations) for their help with and contributions to this project.

Marlinespike Seamanship: An Introduction

Knots, *Bends, and Hitches for Mariners* is a guide prepared by the United States Power Squadrons (USPS) for those with a desire to know more about boating and the marine environment.

Some enterprising human in prehistoric times discovered that twisting long fibers of vegetation together produced a useful tool. Today we call this tool *rope*. Right on the heels of that discovery came the realization that a knot in this primitive rope expanded and enhanced its original purpose, whether that purpose was to make weapons, clothing, or shelter. Working with rope and knots ranks high and early on the list of man's great discoveries. The wheel, fire, cultivation of the soil, the ax, and other tools came thousands of years after rope and knots. Among those early humans were some who not only knew the trick of tying a secure knot but could do it again and again as required. Undoubtedly, those early experts were respected for possessing such knowledge.

Rope and knots have always been associated with watercraft. The first watercraft were probably rafts made from fallen logs tied together with primitive rope and knots. Once humans realized that wind could propel a boat through the water, rope and knots were indispensable in making the concept work. Man's passion to

1

Knots, Bends, and Hitches for Mariners

travel and explore created the need for larger and more complex boats and ships. In the nineteenth century the large clipper ships and fighting ships of the line were driven by thousands of square feet of sail supported and controlled by miles of line with countless knots and splices.

By today's standards, travel by sail was a slow process requiring large crews to run the ships. Life on a sailing ship was characterized by short periods of frantic activity and long periods of waiting for the next frantic action. It was natural for sailors to devote some of their spare time to working with rope and knots. There was always rigging to make and mend. From this utility ropework evolved the decorative and fancy ropework that is so admired today.

The use of knots, bends, and hitches around boats and boating is frequently referred to as *marlinespike seamanship. Webster's Unabridged Dictionary* defines the word *marlinespike* as:

> **mar•line•spike** (mär′lin spīk′), *n.* **1.** An iron rod tapering to a point, used to separate the strands of a rope in splicing. [Written also *marlinspike* and *marling spike.*]

But marlinespike seamanship involves much more than how to use an iron rod to assist in splicing rope. The objective of this guide is to describe the uses of modern rope and knots in recreational boating, to help you be a more knowledgeable boater. The knots, bends, and hitches described here comprise a selection of the most common functional boating knots as well as some interesting decorative knots. We hope that your interest in rope and line management will lead to learning more about USPS and the opportunities offered by this organization.

Marlinespike Seamanship Terminology

It seems that every item or action involved with boating has some special name. The front of a boat is called the *bow* and the rear is called the *stern*. The left side is the *port* side and the right side is the *starboard* side. Messing around with rope, line, knots, bends, and hitches is no exception. For example, you can *tie* a knot, or you can *cast* a knot—it means the exact same thing. In the glossary, you will find the definitions of many of the special words related to marlinespike seamanship. Refer to this glossary frequently as you proceed through this guide. You may also refer to the USPS website to use the master glossary available there. Go to www.usps.org and start exploring.

Marlinespike seamanship terminology is further complicated by the use of regional terms to describe certain aspects of the art. As you may discover, there are a number of detailed references on marlinespike seamanship, and they don't all agree on some of the terms. This guide will use a minimum of technical terms when describing parts of a line and basic rope configurations.

Parts of a Line

Rope is nothing more or less than a thick strong cord made of intertwined strands of fiber, thin wires, leather strips, etc. In a store,

Knots, Bends, and Hitches for Mariners

it is called rope. When rope is used around boats and put to work, it is usually referred to as *line*. To complicate things even more, many lines on a boat have special names. The anchor line is called the *anchor rode*. A sail on a sailboat is positioned relative to the wind using a line called a *sheet*. Of course, there are always exceptions. The rope attached to the bell clapper is called, of all things, the *bell rope*. Isn't tradition wonderful? Finally, although not completely accurate, the two words *line* and *rope* are often used interchangeably.

For the purposes of this guide, we will use the terms *working part* and *bitter end* to describe the parts of a rope. The working part is the part of a rope that is under load. You may find different names, such as the standing part or the running part, used in other books. The bitter end, also known as the end or working end, is the part of a rope that normally carries no load (unless you pull on it), and which hangs out of the knot when you are done. These two terms are sufficient to explain how to tie any knot.

The part of the rope between the working part and the bitter end—that is, the part that is inside the knot—is described by its configuration as you proceed with the steps in the casting of the knot.

Basic Rope Configurations

There are several basic rope configurations that are commonly used in the casting of knots. The most direct example of this is the hitch known as the Round Turn with Two Half Hitches. Not surprisingly, the basic configurations in this case are the round turn and the half hitch, which are among the seven configurations described below. Some of the complex knots in this guide use most of the seven.

Bight

A *bight* is formed when a rope is doubled back on itself (Figure 1). It can be just a few inches long and open, such as the start of a Sheet Bend, or it can be many feet long with no space between the parts of the bight, such as when casting a Bowline on a Bight. A bight is never taken around an object.

4

Marlinespike Seamanship Terminology

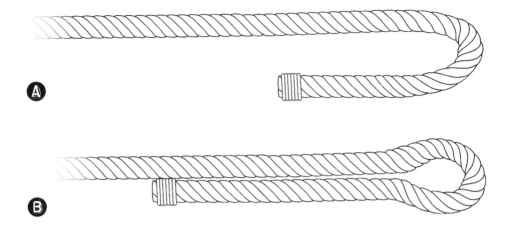

Figure 1. Open (A) and closed (B) bight.

Turn

A *turn* is formed by partially wrapping a rope around an object, such as a pole or another line, with the wrap between 180° and 270° (Figure 2).

Jam Turn

A *jam turn* is a variation of a turn in which you apply tension to the bitter end and pull it over the working part to increase the friction in the configuration (Figure 3). This is done to control the motion of whatever is pulling on the working part of the line. For example, on a boat you would apply a jam turn to a cleat or a pile (piling) to control the motion of the boat.

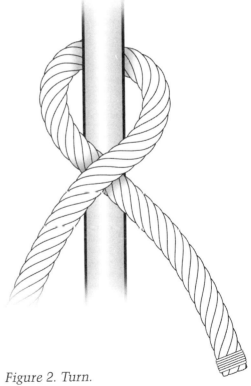

Figure 2. Turn.

Knots, Bends, and Hitches for Mariners

Figure 3. Jam turn.

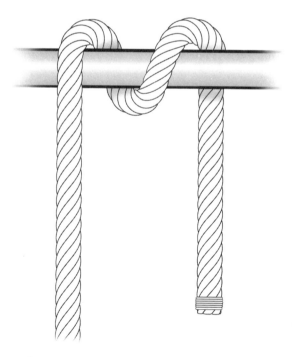

Figure 4. Round turn.

Round Turn

A *round turn* is formed when a rope is wrapped one and a half times (540°) around an object (Figure 4).

Overhand Loop

An *overhand loop* or *forward loop* is made by crossing the bitter end over the working part (Figure 5). This is the first step in a Bowline (pages 46, 47), a Japanese Success Knot (pages 63–64), or a Buntline Hitch (pages 88, 89).

Underhand Loop

An *underhand loop* or *backward loop* is formed by crossing the bitter end under the working part (Figure 6). This is the first step in an Angler's Loop (pages 50, 52–53) or a Jar Sling (pages 95–97).

Figure 5. Overhand loop.   *Figure 6. Underhand loop.*

Knots, Bends, and Hitches for Mariners

Figure 7. Half hitch.

Half Hitch

Use the *half hitch* for attaching a rope to a ring or spar for a right-angle pull. You can also use it in conjunction with a second half hitch or add it to many other knots, such as a Bowline (pages 46, 47), Angler's Loop (pages 50, 52–53), Clove Hitch (pages 80–82, 83), or Constrictor Knot (pages 100, 102–3), to prevent slipping.

To tie a half hitch, first pass the bitter end of the rope around the spar, then tie an Overhand Knot (pages 37, 38) to the working part (Figure 7). Since a half hitch slips easily when applied alone, add a second half hitch after it is drawn up. This will make it quite reliable.

Breaking Strength Versus Working Strength

The *breaking strength* of a line is the load that will cause the line to *part* (on a boat, a line doesn't break, it parts). Some rope manufacturers call this the tensile strength. The *working strength* of a

Marlinespike Seamanship Terminology

line is the safe load you can apply to a certain size and type of rope. In this guide and in common usage, the working strength is one-fifth, or 20%, of the breaking strength.

Knots Weaken Rope

The truth is, any bend or kink in a line weakens it. For example, most splices reduce the line strength by about 10% to 15%, while a Clove Hitch, Bowline, or Sheet Bend reduces the line strength by about 40%. The table below identifies the effects some common knots and splices have on the strength of a straight, unknotted length of line.

EFFECT OF KNOTS ON ROPE STRENGTH

KNOT OR SPLICE	% REDUCTION
Unknotted rope	0
Eye Splice on thimble	10
Long Splice	15
Short Splice	15
Anchor Bend	25
Timber Hitch	30
Round turn	30
Two half hitches	30
Bowline	40
Clove Hitch	40
Sheet Bend	40
Square Knot	55

Knots, Bends, Hitches, and Splices

Knots, bends, hitches, and splices are designed to perform certain jobs. They are all different, with their own special characteristics. Collectively, they are all considered "knots." Thus the word *knot* has both a specific and a generic connotation, and you must ascertain from the context which is meant.

- In its narrow usage, a *knot* puts either a loop or a stopper (lump) in the end of a line. A Bowline (pages

9

Knots, Bends, and Hitches for Mariners

46, 47) is a knot that puts a loop in the end of a line. A Figure-Eight Knot (pages 38, 40) is a stopper in the end of a line and is designed so that the bitter end will not accidentally pass through a block.

- A *bend* attaches two lines together. The Sheet Bend (pages 68–70) is excellent for this application.

- A *hitch* attaches a line to an object. Use a Cleat Hitch (pages 82, 84) to attach a line to a cleat. Use a Clove Hitch (pages 80–82, 83) to attach a line to a pile.

- A *splice* is a permanent rope configuration that prevents a rope end from unraveling (Back Splice, pages 105, 106–7), joins two lines together (Short Splice or Long Splice, pages 113–14 and 114–16), or installs an eye in the end of a line (Eye Splice, pages 116–22).

There are two phases to tying a knot successfully. The first is crossing the parts of the knot in the correct order. The second, almost as important as the first, is tightening or closing the knot properly. You can set up a knot correctly and have all the lines crossing properly, but if you tighten the parts of the knot improperly you may wind up with a totally different knot—one that won't work for you.

Generally speaking, if you tie a knot slowly and avoid sudden, strong jerking motions, you will find it easier to end up with a correct knot. You may need a padded vise to improve the appearance of decorative knots, such as the Monkey's Fist (pages 44–46), Crown Sennit (pages 130, 131), Tack Knot (pages 130, 132, 133–34), and the Star Knot (pages 132, 135–39).

Some knots, such as the Jar Sling (pages 95–97), Turk's Head (pages 126–29), and Star Knot (pages 132, 135–39), require initial loose placement of the strands, then a tightening of the strands to their exact final position. Other knots, such as the Crown Sennit (pages 130, 131) and Three-Strand Cockscomb (pages 143–45), require each set of tucks to be firmly tightened in place as you form the knot. Obviously, the more experience you gain in knot tying, the more successful you will be in producing excellent results.

The knot-tying instructions in this guide are all written for a right-handed person. Reverse all the "hands" if you are left-handed.

10

3

Working with Rope

Marlinespike seamanship involves more than knowledge of knots and splices. This chapter covers rope materials and construction and shows why the large variety of both is important in order to satisfy the many line requirements on a boat. You will also find sections here on cutting, joining, and dyeing rope, as well as necessary information about the care of rope in a marine environment.

Rope Materials

Rope for marine use is made from a wide variety of materials. It is the specific material that determines—for the most part—the properties of a particular type of rope.

- **Nylon** rope (polyamide fiber) is strong, stretches significantly, doesn't rot, doesn't float, and has good resistance to environmental elements, mainly sun and ozone.
- **Polyester** rope (Dacron) is strong, has medium stretch, doesn't rot, doesn't float, and has good resistance to environmental elements.
- **Polypropylene** (olefin) and **polyethylene** ropes have medium strength, low stretch, don't rot, *do* float, and are degraded by sunlight and ozone.

11

Knots, Bends, and Hitches for Mariners

- **Aramid fiber** (Kevlar) rope is super-strong, has almost no stretch, doesn't rot, doesn't float, and has good resistance to environmental elements; however, it is easily damaged by tight bending and kinking.

- **Various high-tech fibers** (Spectra 1000, Dyneema SK75, Technora, and Vectran) are all extremely strong, have very low stretch, don't rot, and have good resistance to environmental elements. Spectra and Dyneema are high-tenacity polyethylene, and do float, unless they have a Dacron cover, in which case they may not float. Technora is a high-tenacity copolymer, and Vectran is a liquid-crystal polymer; they do not float. Some rope manufacturers combine high-tech fibers to enhance rope properties.

Most rope manufacturers attach their own brand names to their products. This makes it difficult to determine exactly what you are buying. For high-performance rope products, it is best to

PROPERTIES OF ⅜-INCH ROPE

ROPE MATERIAL	ROPE CONSTRUCTION	COVER FIBER	CORE FIBER
Nylon	Laid	Nylon	—
Nylon	Double-braid	Nylon	Nylon
Dacron	Laid	Polyester	—
Dacron	Single-braid	Polyester	—
Dacron	Double-braid	Polyester	Polyester
Dacron	Parallel-core	Polyester	Polyester
Poly	Single-braid	Polypropylene	—
Spectra	Single-braid	4	—
Spectra	Double-braid	Polyester	4
Technora	Double-braid	Polyester	5
Kevlar	Parallel-core	Polyester	Aramid
Vectran	Single-braid	6	—

Notes:
1. Strengths based on ⅜-inch ropes, averaged for several manufacturers.
2. Safe working load (SWL) based on 20% of breaking strength.
3. Maximum stretch values differ with age of rope, moisture content, and temperature.

Working with Rope

select from the manufacturer's catalog, picking the specific properties you need. The table lists some of the more common ropes and their average properties.

Rope Construction

Marine rope in the days of sail was commonly available in only one configuration: twisted three-strand (or laid). Now, the great variety of choices can be confusing. The four most common rope constructions are laid, single-braid, double-braid, and parallel core. The construction has some influence on the properties of the rope.

Laid Rope

Laid rope, or three-strand rope, has three components: fibers, yarns, and strands (Figure 8). The three strands are the outside part of the construction, or the part you see. In right-laid rope, the strands wind up and to the right when the rope is held vertically.

BREAKING STRENGTH[1] (LBS.)	SAFE WORKING LOAD[2] (LBS.)	MAXIMUM STRETCH AT SWL[3] (%)	FLOATS	ROTS
4,400	880	18	No	No
4,900	980	8	No	No
3,900	780	6	No	No
4,200	810	5	No	No
4,400	880	4	No	No
5,500	1,100	3	No	No
1,900	380	3	Yes	No
19,000	3,800	2	Yes	No
10,000	2,000	2	No	No
11,800	2,360	2	No	No
12,500	2,500	1	No	No
16,800	3,360	1	No	No

4. Spectra is high-tenacity polyethylene.
5. Technora is high-tenacity copolymer.
6. Vectran is liquid-crystal polymer.

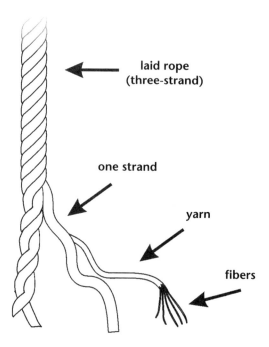

Figure 8. Three-strand rope.

Each strand is made of a number of yarns, which wind up and to the left. Each yarn is made of fibers, which wind up and to the right. The result is a relatively stable construction designed to not spring apart when cut (although the rope ends should be *whipped* to keep them from unraveling). This construction stretches the most and is also more prone to kink (if not handled properly) and to wear on the outer fibers.

Single-Braid Rope

Single-braid rope comprises bundles of fibers running diagonally in both directions that are woven or braided together where they cross (Figure 9). It is stronger than laid rope, stretches less, and is generally easier to handle. It also is more wear resistant.

Double-Braid Rope

Double-braid rope often appears the same as single-braid rope, but inside the braided cover is a smaller braided rope core (Figure 10). The properties are often similar to single-braid rope, although sometimes the double-braid product is stronger and has less

Working with Rope

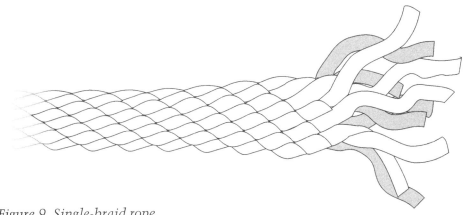

Figure 9. Single-braid rope.

stretch. Also, some rope manufacturers offer special double-braid products constructed with a wear-resistant polyester-braid cover over a braided core of less durable but enormously strong high-tech fiber. The properties of these special ropes come from the core and are usually ultrastrong with very low stretch.

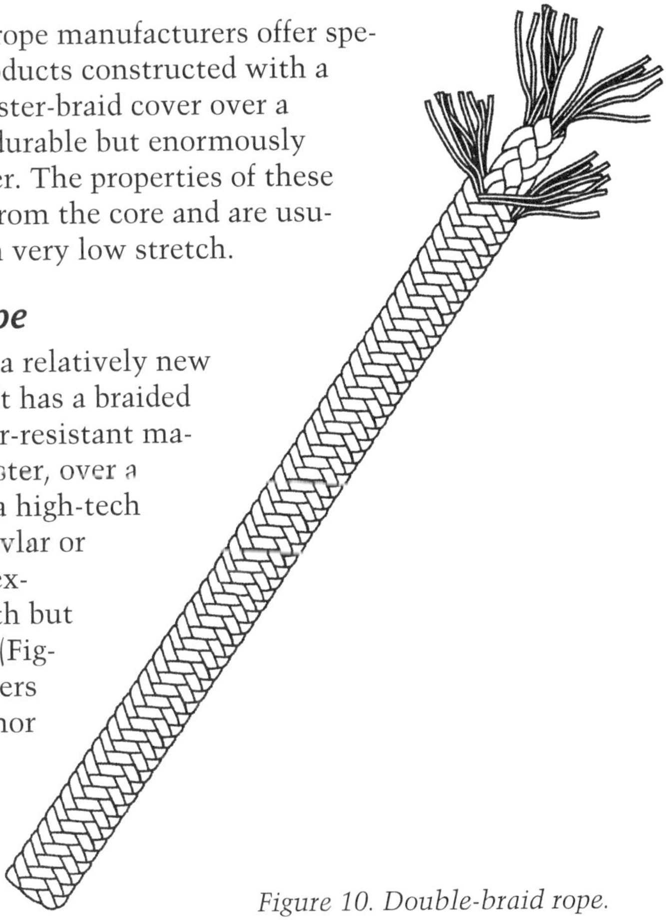

Parallel-Core Rope

Parallel-core rope is a relatively new rope configuration. It has a braided cover made of a wear-resistant material, such as polyester, over a core of polyester or a high-tech material, such as Kevlar or Spectra, which has extremely high strength but is somewhat fragile (Figure 11). The core fibers are neither twisted nor braided. The integrity of the rope depends entirely on the braided cover, while the

Figure 10. Double-braid rope.

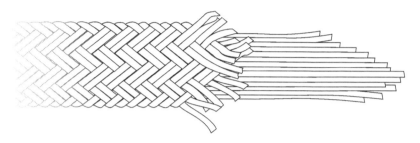

Figure 11. Parallel-core rope.

properties of the rope come entirely from the high-strength, low-stretch core. The stretch is generally so low that the entire load is taken by the core.

Common Rope Uses Aboard

Selecting the best rope for a particular use on a boat is a two-step process. First, you should list, in the order of their importance, the rope properties needed for the application. Then, the second step is relatively easy. Go to a table of rope properties, such as the one on pages 12–13, and select the rope product whose material and construction properties best suit your needs.

- **Anchor rodes** need high strength, high stretch, rot resistance, and they should not float. Laid nylon is the rope of choice.

- **Dock lines** need high strength, medium stretch, rot resistance, and abrasion resistance. The best rope choice is either single- or double-braid rope of either nylon or Dacron fiber.

- A **sheet** is a line on a sailboat used to control the angle of a sail to the wind. It is either handheld, or winch controlled and hand tailed. The properties needed are high strength, low stretch, rot resistance, abrasion resistance, and ease of handling. For these properties, the rope of choice is Dacron fiber double-braid with a "fuzzy" cover braid.

- **Halyards** are lines on a sailboat used to raise and

Working with Rope

hold the sails up. The properties needed for a halyard are very high strength, very low stretch, rot resistance, and resistance to environmental elements. For racing sailors, the ultimate line choice is a high-tech rope with Kevlar, Spectra 1000, Dyneema SK75, Technora, or Vectran, all of which have catalog properties of high strength and low stretch. Cruising sailors might select a lower-cost line such as a Dacron double-braid or Dacron parallel-core rope.

- **Waterskiing lines and painters** are both towlines. Curiously, the most important property here is low stretch, followed by flotation and adequate strength. Polypropylene (or polyethylene) braided line has all the required properties.

Cutting Rope

Choosing the best way to cut marine rope depends on two factors: the type of rope, and the tools available. Meltable rope can be cut with a heat-gun rope cutter or a hot knife. Any fiber rope can be cut with a sharp knife or razor blade. The most common cutting methods are described below.

Cold Cutting

Occasionally, it is desirable to *cold-cut* the end of a rope so that the ends are not sealed and the line can be easily unlaid in preparation for a splice or a knot, such as the Matthew Walker Knot (pages 110–12). If you use a new safety razor blade, the cut will be rapid and clean, with unmelted ends. Then you can unlay the strands as needed. Before cutting, wrap the cut zone tightly with masking tape to prevent unlaying of the individual strands. Cut through the middle of the tape zone, cutting both the tape and the rope.

Heat Cutting

You can heat-cut meltable marine rope either by using an electrical tool or heating a blade. Electrical heat-gun rope cutters (Figure 12) are generally available wherever rope is sold. A heat-gun cutter makes angle cuts as easily as straight cuts. Mounting a medium-size spring clamp in a table vise is useful as an extra "hand" so you can keep the rope taut in the cutting area and still have a hand to hold the cutting tool.

If electricity is not available to power a heat-cutting blade, such as in an emergency, you can use a gas flame to heat a knife or tool-held safety razor blade. This method accomplishes the same purpose as outlined above, but it is more cumbersome and perhaps less precise. Also, the heat may damage the blade.

When using any heat-cutting equipment make sure you are in a well-ventilated area. Wear a heat-resistant glove on one hand and grasp the cutter in the other hand. Heat the blade in short (1- to 3-second) bursts of heat to control the cut. This lessens the chance of unintentionally burning adjacent strands of rope.

The heat-cutting method produces a useful secondary result. As the rope is cut, it melts, automatically preventing unlaying. Also, if you use a gloved hand to hold the ends of the freshly

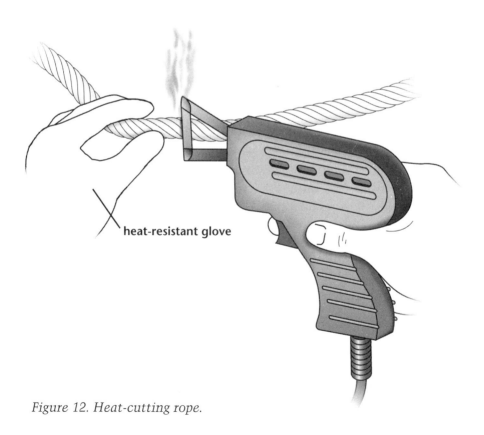

Figure 12. Heat-cutting rope.

Working with Rope

heated rope together, they will melt together. If the edges of the cut or heat-melted joint are slightly frayed, you can use your gloved fingers to twist the end, thus turning the frayed end toward the core of the rope. But you must do this within seconds of making the cut.

Last but not least, be careful! Melted rope is very hot and can cause severe burns.

Safety hint: It is a good practice to keep a fresh lubricated blade or a sailor's (rigging) knife in your boat or dinghy. With this blade you can sever a line that otherwise could not be released—for example, on an improperly tied boat about to be sunk by a rising tide.

Joining Rope

Using Heat

In *decorative* knotting, where the rope and knot will never carry a load, such as a rope border around a picture frame, joining can be done by using a heat gun. Heated line melts fast, and once the heat source is removed, it cools rapidly. With practice, you will easily perfect your joining technique.

When joining, keep the heat blade clean by scraping it with an old safety razor blade between cuts. Use short bursts of heat (1 to 3 seconds) to make a cut and also to melt the two ends of the line together.

Hidden joints can be made anywhere in the production of a long Sennit or a Cockscomb (pages 143–45). You can also join together lines of different diameters, as will be illustrated later when describing the production of the Bell Rope Sennit (pages 140–42).

Warning! Never use a heat gun to join rope that will carry a load. A heated joint will not hold.

Using Glue

Glue is generally not used for joining rope because most glues are water soluble, and the joint could be weakened by moisture. The gluing process also discolors the rope. However, epoxy cement or white glues may be very useful in decorative line work, such as preparing knot display boards or marlinespike seamanship teaching aids. For example, the final stages of some knots, such as a plug in a Tack Knot or Star Knot (see Figure 13), may be secured by white glue, especially when no stress will be placed on the knot and no exposure to water is expected.

With that said, if you can't use the heat-melt process to secure a knot to another line or object for decorative purposes, consider using epoxy glue. Use only enough to do the job and to avoid an unsightly appearance. After applying the glue, use a heavy weight or spring clamp to stabilize the joint for at least 24 hours. Remove any excess glue at the edges with a sharp scalpel or razor blade.

Several examples of complex decorative knots are shown below. Each is described elsewhere in the book.

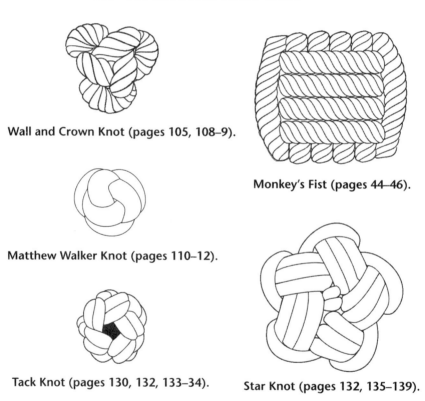

Wall and Crown Knot (pages 105, 108–9).

Monkey's Fist (pages 44–46).

Matthew Walker Knot (pages 110–12).

Tack Knot (pages 130, 132, 133–34).

Star Knot (pages 132, 135–139).

Figure 13. Examples of complex decorative knots.

Dyeing Rope

Changing the color of rope is an effective method of identifying a particular segment of a knot. Adding color to decorative knots also adds to the beauty of the finished product. However, use dyed rope

Working with Rope

only for decoration as the dye will change the properties of the rope. For example, some nylon rope will stiffen after the dyeing process is complete, and all rope will lose strength when dyed. But for decorative purposes, these changes are not a problem. The dyeing instructions that follow will give you some surprising results.

Equipment for Dyeing Rope

Listed below is the basic equipment you will need for dyeing rope:

- A pan of sufficient size used for dyeing only.
- Spaghetti tongs for handling hot rope.
- A flat board for stirring line while in the dye.
- Good-quality dyes in the desired colors.

Dyeing Method

Follow these step-by-step instructions to dye 10 feet of nylon rope:

1. Fill a pan with 8 cups of hot water and bring to a boil.
2. Add 4 tablespoons of dye; stir to dissolve.
3. Place the rope in the boiling dye-water mixture; allow for approximately 20% shrinkage of rope during the dyeing process.
4. Stir the rope slowly and continuously for 2 to 5 minutes, depending on the depth of color desired. (It is best to dye rope slightly darker than you want it to appear in the knot, as the color will lighten as the rope dries and sunlight will cause fading.)
5. Remove the dyed rope from the boiling water with the tongs and rinse in cool water.
6. Pull the rope through a clean, dry cloth to damp-dry it.
7. Stretch the rope to its original 10 feet and allow it to air-dry for 24 hours.
8. Clean the pan with cold water and a sponge immediately after each procedure to avoid chemical damage to the pan.

Knots, Bends, and Hitches for Mariners

- Allow the rope to dry completely before using it to cast a knot.

Line Ends (Whipping Lines)

Whipping is a general term covering the treatment of the ends of a line to prevent them from unraveling or fraying. There are many methods for whipping a line, with varying degrees of effectiveness. They are most commonly used on the whole rope end (Figure 14). For splicing, and when making decorative knots, it is also often necessary to whip the individual rope strands to keep them from unraveling. When splicing and temporarily whipping the strand ends with tape, you may want to taper the tape to a point to facilitate slipping the end between the other rope strands.

Following are several methods for whipping a line:

- **Durable tape**, such as vinyl or reinforced banding tape, can be used for whipping, although the results aren't long-lasting. Wrap the line with wide tape—three wraps around the line works best—then cut the tape and line.

- **Meltable rope** such as nylon, Dacron, and polypropylene can be heat-sealed on the ends. The best procedure for this is to securely wrap the line with wide masking tape at the location of the cut. Cut the line in the middle of the tape. Melt the exposed line end with a propane torch; it works better than a match. Be careful—you want to melt the line, not set it on fire. You should aim to create a "melt plug" at least $1/16$ inch thick at the end of the line. The tape will keep the plug the same size as the line. After the plug cools, remove the tape. Properly

Figure 14. Whipping.

Working with Rope

done, this method will seal the end of the line and prevent unraveling for years.

- **Plastic shrink sleeves** are available at most marine stores. Select a size appropriate for your line size. Slip the sleeve over your line end and heat the sleeve according to the package instructions to shrink it in place on your line. This system works on any line material and is a long-lasting way to whip line ends.

- **Liquid whipping** is an air-drying liquid into which you dip the end of your line. When it dries, or cures, you should have an effective coating on the end of your line to prevent unraveling. This system also works with any line material.

- **True whipping** with *small stuff* (heavy string or twine) is still the most-attractive, lowest-cost, most-effective, and longest-lasting method of pro-

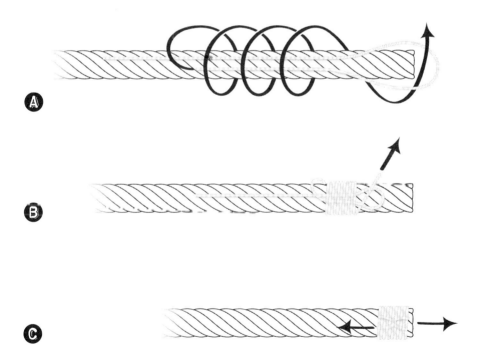

Figure 15. True whipping.

Knots, Bends, and Hitches for Mariners

tecting your line ends from unraveling. Unlike the other methods, true whipping can actually reduce the size of the whipped end so the end will easily pass through any opening large enough for the working part of the line. Use either waxed, 40# test, three-strand Dacron twine, or 50# to 80# test, Dacron braided fishing line for small stuff.

Start with an open bight in the small stuff, lengthwise to the line, with the loop end of the bight overlapping the end of the line. Wind the small stuff tightly around the line until the length of the wrapped section is equal to the diameter of the line (Figure 15A). Insert the end of the small stuff through the loop of the bight and pull the end tight (Figure 15B). Hold the last turn with your fingers to keep the turns tight and pull the exposed small stuff end from under the other end of the turns, drawing the loop of the bight and the other end of the small stuff back under the turns of small stuff (Figure 15C). Clip off the small stuff ends close to the turns. The result will be a tightly wrapped whipping with no visible knots or ends.

Seizing Lines

Seizing is the tying together of two parallel lines with small stuff to prevent relative lengthwise motion between the lines (Figure 16). You might use one seizing to tie the bitter end of a line to the working part of the line to ensure that a knot doesn't *capsize* or loosen. Or you can use up to five spaced seizings to trap a thimble in a line bight instead of using an Eye Splice.

Start a seizing with a small-stuff Clove Hitch (pages 80–83) around one of the lines. Proceed by tightly wrapping ten to fifteen turns of small stuff around both lines, binding them together. To tighten these wraps, take three or four crossing turns between the lines and around the first ten to fifteen turns, pulling each crossing turn tight. Then use a Reef Knot (pages 76–77) to tie off the bitter end of the small stuff to the bitter end of the original Clove Hitch.

Working with Rope

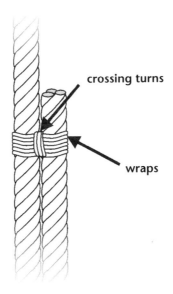

Figure 16. Seizing.

Care of Line

Lines wear out and/or fail for a variety of reasons. The following guidelines will help you keep your lines in good condition:

- **Avoid overloading.** All rope has a rated strength or safe working load as well as a breaking strength. However, rope doesn't have to be loaded even close to its breaking strength to be overloaded and permanently damaged. Signs of rope damage include a noticeable reduction in the size of the rope, a noticeable permanent increase in the length of the rope, or an increase in the stiffness of the rope. Replace rope that exhibits any of these warning signs.

- **Avoid overheating.** Lines in storm conditions fail when they overheat and melt internally. This occurs when high winds and storm waves create forces on the boat that stretch and overload the dock lines. Follow-up studies of failed dock lines from the 2004 Florida hurricanes revealed that some of the lines

25

Knots, Bends, and Hitches for Mariners

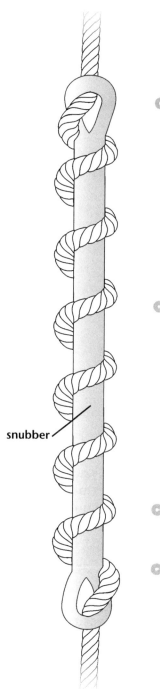

had melted inside. The age-old sailor's trick of doubling up the dock lines before a storm has some obvious merit. You might also consider using heavier dock lines.

- **Avoid shock loading.** The most common instances of shock loading (sudden, heavy loads) of lines on a boat involve anchoring and tying off at a dock. You can reduce shock loading by using the proper type of line. For example, laid nylon is a good choice for an anchor rode because of its natural high stretch. You can "shock load proof" dock lines by installing rubber snubbers (Figure 17).

- **Avoid kinking.** Laid line sometimes kinks in a characteristic way when it is twisted against the normal lay of the line (called a *hockle*; Figure 18). Never use line that is in this condition. You can usually remove a hockle by twisting it with the lay of the line and flexing the strands to allow them to settle back into their normal positions. Braided line is more difficult to kink and also more difficult to unkink.

- **Avoid sharp bends.** Sharp bends weaken all lines. Avoid creating a sharp bend in a rope eye by using a *thimble*; Figure 19.

- **Avoid harsh chemicals.** The majority of modern marine ropes are resistant to most common chemicals, but why take the chance? Protect your lines from contact with harsh chemicals; try not to splash them with battery acid, acetone, peroxide, etc.

Figure 17. A rubber snubber in a dock line.

Figure 18. Hockle in laid line. *Figure 19. Thimble.*

- **Protect your line from environmental elements.** Sunlight and ozone are both weathering agents and can affect lines, especially those made of polypropylene and polyethylene. Keep unused line properly stowed to minimize exposure to these agents.

- **Uncoil new line carefully to prevent kinks.** Roll the line out of the coil or spool to avoid introducing kinks in the line.

- **Protect lines from chafe.** Wherever possible, route lines to avoid rubbing contact with hard objects— especially hard, sharp-edged objects and most especially hard, sharp-edged, and rough objects. A good example of the latter is a dock line rubbing on the raw edge of a concrete pier. If this situation is unavoidable, then be sure to use effective chafing gear to protect the line. Keep in mind that chafing gear will wear through also, so be sure to check it regularly and replace when necessary.

Most marine stores sell chafe sleeves made of

leather, plastic, or rubber. Sew, tie, or tape the sleeves in place according to the product instructions, making sure to cover the length of line where chafe could be a problem. Also ensure the vessel's lines are in place and adjusted to their final settings before installing the chafing gear.

You can chafe-protect small dock lines (½ inch, ⅝ inch, and ¾ inch) by using a similarly sized garden hose. Split the hose lengthwise and hold it in place with reinforced tape or electrical wire ties.

- **Keep lines clean.** Lines do get dirty and become contaminated with chemicals and grit. When this happens, lay them out and hose them with clean, fresh water. If they are stained with dirt or mildew, you can clean them in a washing machine as follows:

First, coil the line carefully in neat coils about 15 inches in diameter. Next, tie the coils securely together at 0°, 90°, 180°, and 270° with several turns

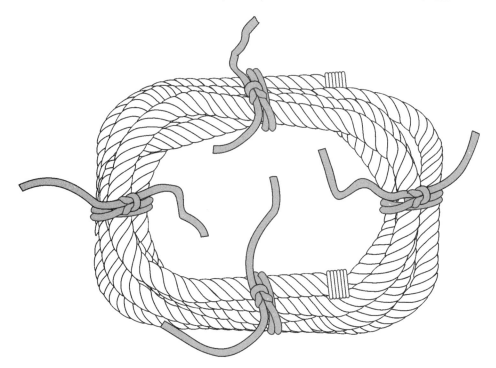

Figure 20. A rope coiled for washing.

of small stuff securely knotted (Figure 20). Set the washing machine on a medium agitation cycle with warm (not hot) water and use laundry soap with no bleach. Do not place the rope coil over the washer "agitator." After washing, cut off the small stuff and hang the clean line to air-dry.

Proper Line Storage

All line requires proper storage. Following are guidelines for storing line properly.

- **Don't store wet lines.** Modern marine line will not rot, but it will mildew. Dry your lines before stowing them.
- **Coil line carefully for stowage.** Never coil line around your arm like a clothesline. Instead, hold the coils in one hand. As you add coils with the other hand, twist the line with your fingers so the coils lie flat against each other. If one end of the line is

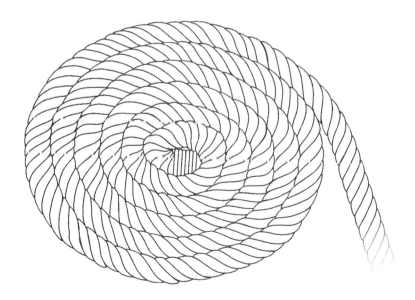

Figure 21. A Flemish Coil shows other boaters you are a skilled marlinespike mariner.

Knots, Bends, and Hitches for Mariners

attached to something (like a cleat), coil the line from the fixed end toward the loose end. This will allow the uncoiled line to rotate as you twist it with your fingers to coil it. This process works with both laid and braided line.

- **Coil lines for ready usage.** Lines for ready use, such as dock lines, should be coiled and tied off with part of the coiled line to keep the coils from becoming tangled. Special hooks are available for hanging these coils in the cockpit area of the boat.

- **Stow extra line for maximum show-off potential.** Stowing extra line on a pier is an opportunity to show the other boaters that you are a skilled marlinespike mariner. When you tie off to a cleat on a pier, you will always have extra line. Rather than winding up the excess on the cleat (amateurish and ugly), or just leaving the excess in a pile on the pier (dangerous), coil the excess in a flat, circular coil or mat (known as a Flemish Coil; Figure 21) on the pier. It will dry quickly this way, passersby will not trip on it, and it just plain looks good.

Marlinespike Seamanship Tools

Every profession, business, or trade has its tools to do the job a bit better or more easily. Line work and knot casting are no exceptions. The following tools and supplies frequently are needed for working with line and tying knots. Many other specialized tools are available if you are working with sails, double-braid line, or wire.

- A **sailor's knife** with a high-quality stainless steel blade. This tool is also called a rigging knife (Figure 22).

- **Fids** are used to push or pull parts of a line. You can purchase metal and plastic fids in various sizes at most marine supply stores (Figure 23). Plastic fids tend to deteriorate after prolonged use. Fids with hollow shafts may be used to splice double-braid nylon line (Figure 24). They are also useful for making Monkey's Fists (pages 44–46), Tack Knots (pages 130, 132,

Working with Rope

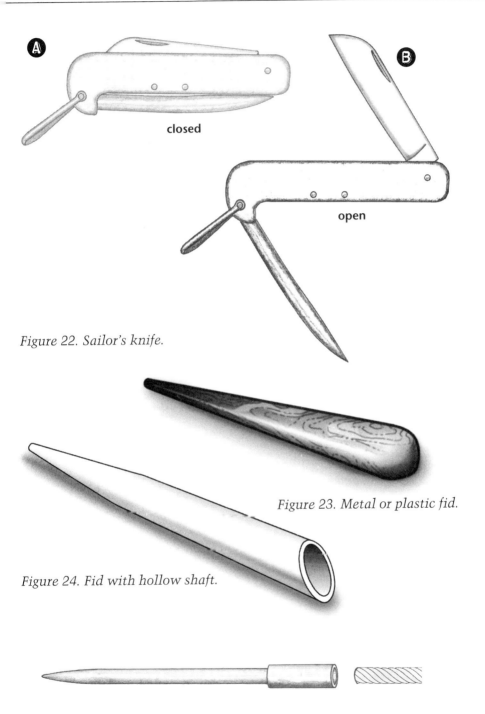

Figure 22. Sailor's knife.

Figure 23. Metal or plastic fid.

Figure 24. Fid with hollow shaft.

Figure 25. Metal fid made from a steel nail.

Knots, Bends, and Hitches for Mariners

133–34), and Star Knots (pages 135–39). You can make your own small metal fid for use with ⅛-inch-diameter braided nylon line (Figure 25). Start with a good quality 10d steel nail, 3 inches long and $5/32$-inch diameter. Cut off the head with a hacksaw, grind the point to a snub nose, and polish the shank and point of the nail. Insert the blunt end of the nail halfway into a ¾-inch-long, 8 AWG noninsulated wire connector and solder in place. This improvised, hollow end fid is ideal for making Turk's Heads (pages 126–29).

- A **kebab skewer** is ideal for pushing a segment of line into a confined space (Figure 26).

- **Hemostats** (surgical instruments) work great as fids (Figure 27). The smooth ends of the small, curved or straight mosquito hemostat and the larger, regular

Figure 26. A kebab skewer for pushing line into a hollow metal fid.

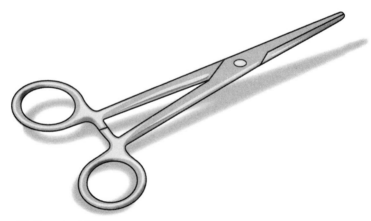

Figure 27. Surgical hemostat.

Working with Rope

hemostat let you separate the rope strands. Then use the hemostat to grasp the end of the line and pull it through the separated strands.

- **Spring clamps** of all sizes are helpful for holding knots in desired positions or in molding knots to a more desirable shape (Figure 28). Clamps act as a "third hand" to help with work. These clamps are also available as locking clamps with ratchet action so they hold very tightly in almost any desired position while the lines making the knot are moved.

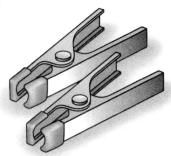

Figure 28. Spring clamps.

- **Sailmaker's needles** of several sizes are used primarily for mending sailcloth. They are also useful when whipping or seizing line (Figure 29).

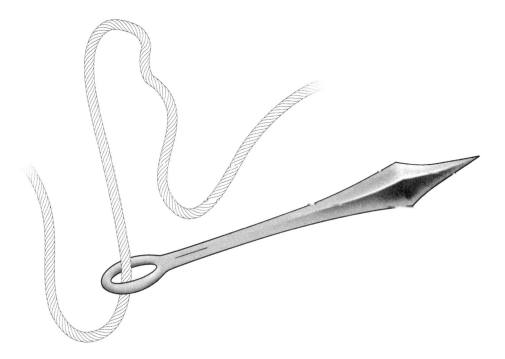

Figure 29. Sailmaker's needle.

33

Knots, Bends, and Hitches for Mariners

- A **sailmaker's palm** is a broad leather strip with an indented socket that is sized to fit your palm. Wear this tool around the palm of your hand to protect the side of the hand and your little finger, thumb, and palm while pushing needles into sailcloth and seizing line (Figure 30).

- **Dowels** of various sizes should be available. When casting a Turk's Head (pages 126–29), you can use a dowel as a template in the center so that the final knot can be drawn up tightly. (A drop of white glue on the inside of the knot at the point of start/finish is useful to prevent the strands from unwinding.)

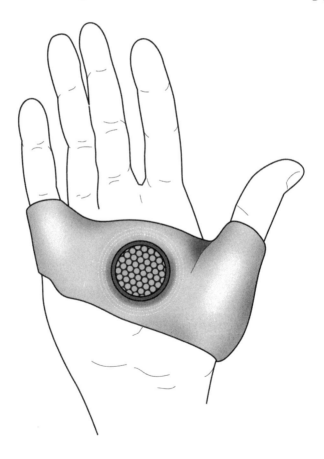

Figure 30. Sailmaker's palm.

- A **measuring tape** lets you determine specific lengths of line.
- A **lead weight** is used for loading a Monkey's Fist (pages 44–46).
- **Masking tape** prevents unlaying during splicing.
- A **toolbox** is good for storage and transport of tools.
- A **toggle**, a removable wooden pin, can be used in place of a loop on a slip knot. The toggle serves as a mechanism for rapid release of the knot and is useful in situations in which the knot might jam if it gets wet. An excellent way to prepare a toggle is to attach twine to one end so that it can be permanently fastened to the working part of the line in the approximate location in which it will be used. Figure 31 shows a toggle attached to the line.

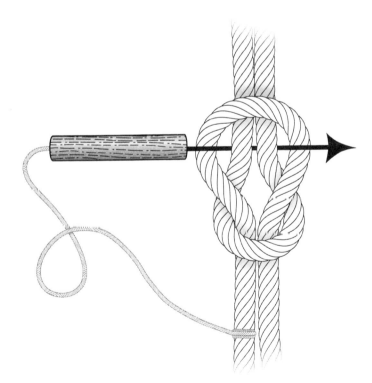

Figure 31. A toggle attached to a line.

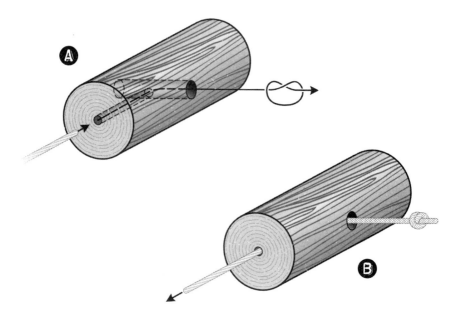

Figure 32. Creating a toggle.

One way to create a toggle is to drill a hole in the center of the length of the round wooden dowel, from one end to a little more than half the length. Make the hole slightly larger in diameter than the twine being used. Drill a second hole, of greater diameter, across the diameter of the toggle from one side to the other as shown in Figure 32A. Insert the twine into the first hole until you see the end in the crossing hole. Then, use a toothpick to push the twine at right angles out the opposite crossing hole. Pull the twine end out and tie an overhand stopper knot in the end of the twine (Figure 32B). Finally, pull it back into the center of the toggle to hide it.

4

Knots

In the narrow sense of the word, knots are of two classes: those that create a stopper (or lump) in the end of a line so the bitter end can't accidentally pass through an opening, such as in a block; and those that form a loop in the end of a line. The knots in this chapter incorporate many of the seven basic rope configurations discussed in Chapter 2.

Rope Ends (Stopper Knots)

Overhand Knot

The Overhand Knot shown in Figure 33 is the simplest of all knots and the first step in many more complicated knots. It is frequently used as a stopper knot. It is small, jams easily, and is difficult to untie if drawn up tight. To tie it, make an overhand loop and pass the bitter end under and up through the loop. The real value of the Overhand Knot is its potential use in other knots (see, for example, the Blood Knot on pages 41–42).

Slipped Overhand Knot (Slip Knot)

The Slip Knot is considered a stopper knot that can be quickly loosened by pulling on the bitter end, thereby removing the loop.

37

Knots, Bends, and Hitches for Mariners

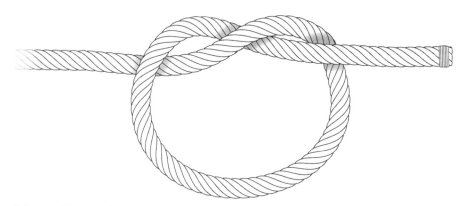

Figure 33. Overhand Knot.

This is the only knot properly called a Slip Knot. All others with a similar motif are properly referred to as "slipped knots."

Using a Slip Knot to tie a stopper in the end of a string, twine, or thin rope is rapid and convenient. It is excellent when you need to untie the stopper quickly, such as when cinching a load under pressure that is firmed down with multiple half hitches.

To tie the Slip Knot, start with an overhand loop (Figure 34A). Instead of pulling the bitter end through the loop (making an Overhand Knot), pull a short bight of the bitter end through the loop (Figures 34A and 34B) leaving enough bitter end protruding from the knot for you pull when you want to release the knot (Figure 34C).

As seen in Figure 34D, you can use the Slip Knot as a quick stopper for a line passed through a grommet in a sail, tarpaulin, or boat cover. The knot won't slip easily (especially when wet), but a firm tug on the bitter end will release it.

Figure-Eight Knot

The Figure-Eight Knot is a better stopper because it is somewhat bulkier than the Overhand Knot. It is also less likely to jam. To cast a Figure-Eight Knot, follow the overhand method, but go 180° farther in the last tuck as shown in Figures 35A, 35B, and 35C.

Stevedore Knot

The Stevedore Knot is a Figure-Eight Knot with an extra turn. It is also known as a Heaving Line Knot. What it lacks in weight, as

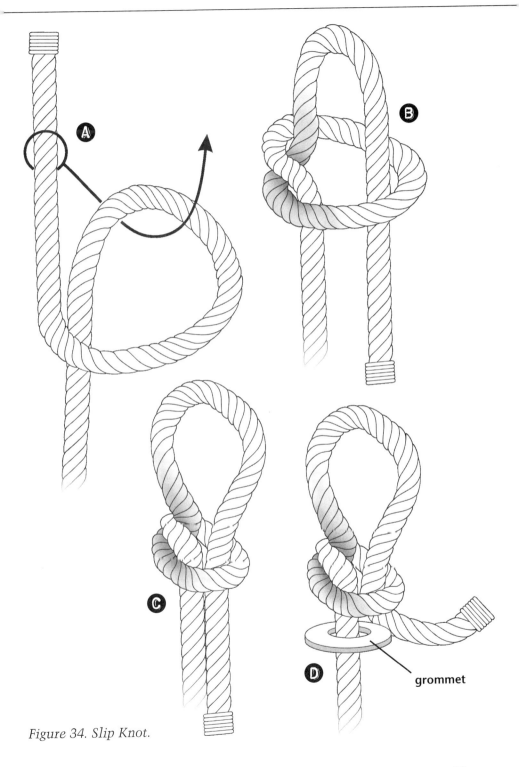

Figure 34. Slip Knot.

Knots, Bends, and Hitches for Mariners

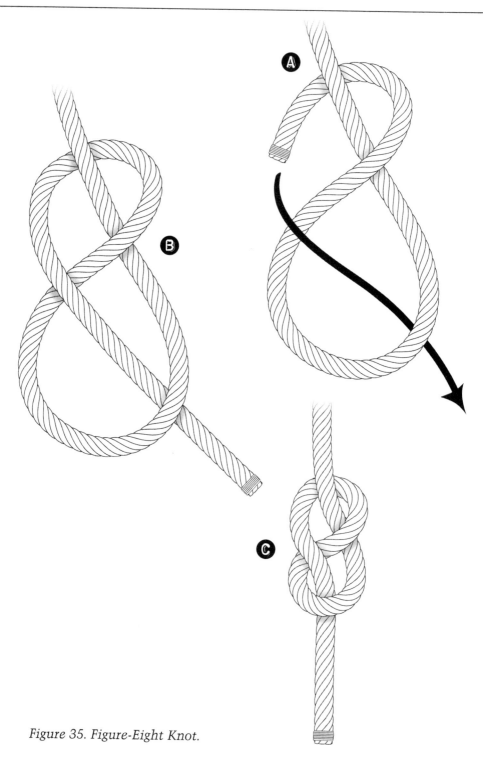

Figure 35. Figure-Eight Knot.

40

Knots

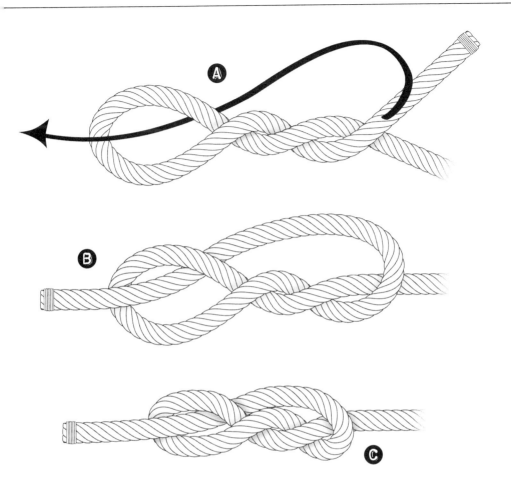

Figure 36. Stevedore Knot.

compared to the Monkey's Fist (pages 44–46) for example, it gains in speed and ease of tying. Near the end of the rope, make a closed bight and twist the loop three half turns while holding (seizing) the bitter end and the working part, then feed the bitter end back through the loop (Figure 36A). Lastly, pull the end up to form the knot as in Figures 36B and 36C. This knot unties easily.

Blood Knot

Occasionally you will need a stopper knot larger than that provided by an Overhand Knot. The Blood Knot, which is also decorative, is ideal for this. Make an overhand loop. Pass the bitter end under and up through the loop once and then again as in Figure

41

Knots, Bends, and Hitches for Mariners

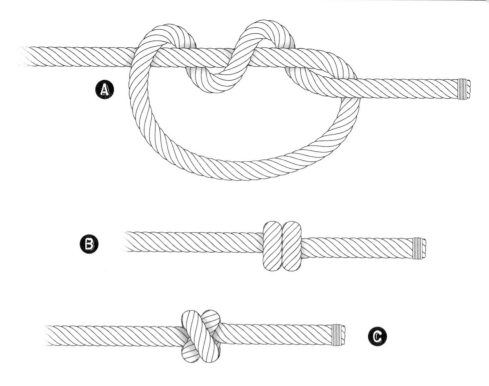

Figure 37. Blood Knot.

37A. Slowly draw the ends up tight. To ensure the final configuration, gently lift the left loop over the right as tightening progresses. Figure 37B shows the front of the knot and Figure 37C shows the back of the knot.

Heaving Line Knot

Occasionally, you will need a weighted line end in order to heave a line a greater distance than is possible with an unweighted end. (The Monkey's Fist is the best method, but it must be prepared ahead of time—there may not be time to tie a Monkey's Fist in an emergency.) The Heaving Line Knot shown in Figure 38 can be prepared rapidly in the end of any small line.

To tie the Heaving Line Knot, form two bights approximately 6 feet from the end as in Figure 38A. Pass the bitter end through the first bight, around behind the first bight, through the second bight, and then wrap it around all the legs of both bights for about ten turns (Figure 38B) until the leftover line end is very near the

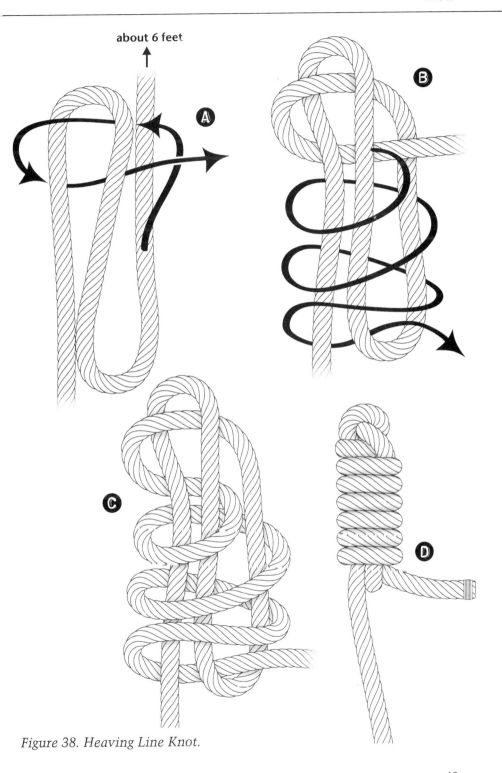

Figure 38. Heaving Line Knot.

loop of the second bight (Figure 38C). Then, pass the bitter end through the second bight, and draw the entire knot tight by pulling on the bitter end and the working part until a heavy and bulky end is formed as in Figure 38D.

This knot can be tricky to tie. Don't wait for an emergency to try it for the first time.

Monkey's Fist

When there is a need to heave a line more than 50 feet, a Monkey's Fist solves the problem.

Start a Monkey's Fist with 6 feet of ⅜-inch nylon rope. Make four turns of continuous line over two fingers (Figure 39A), with

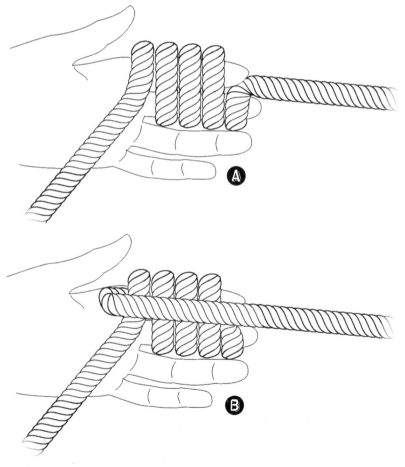

Figure 39. Monkey's Fist.

Knots

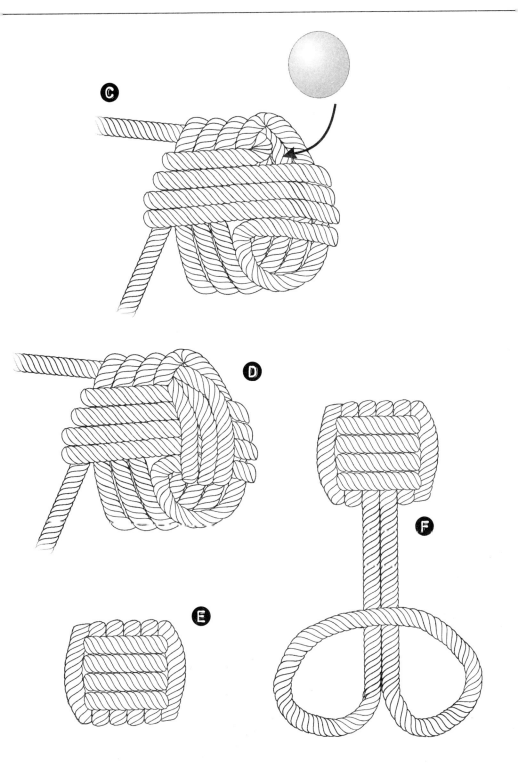

45

Knots, Bends, and Hitches for Mariners

the fingers spread far enough apart to allow the bitter end of the
rope to pass between the fingers. Then make four more turns at
right angles to the first turns, as shown in Figure 39B, and gently
pull the rope off your hand while holding the general shape. Insert
a 1-inch-diameter steel or lead ball in the loose knot (Figure 39C).
Next, make another four turns around the second set of turns, but
bring the bitter end of the rope inside the original set of four turns
as seen in Figure 39D.

Pull the knot tight, slowly and lightly at first, then more
tightly as the last tucks are reached. Use a padded vise for final
cubical shaping (Figure 39E).

The knot may be ended in a couple of ways: you can join the
two bitter ends of the Monkey's Fist by seizing or splicing, or at
the start, you can make a loop (seized or spliced) and hide it in the
knot along with the metal ball as you proceed (Figure 39F).

Loop Knots

The loop knots in this section begin with the basic Bowline and
progress through some interesting and exotic knots with up to
three loops. If you use these knots on your boat, keep a copy of this
guide handy for the illustrated, step-by-step casting instructions.

Bowline

The Bowline is the most useful of all knots aboard a boat. A Bowline, or one of its variations, makes a temporary loop anywhere in
a line. Used on a ring, spar, or cleat, and properly formed, it will
not capsize. It is strong, resists slipping, and is easy to untie.
When wet, a Slipped Bowline reduces the difficulty of untying a
Bowline under constant pressure.

Tie the Bowline by forming an overhand loop as in Figure
40A, through which the bitter end of the line goes up from the
back (Figure 40B), around behind the working part, and back down
through the formed loop. Always shape the knot and tighten
firmly (Figure 40C). Note that the Bowline is a combination of an
overhand loop and a bight and is cast in that manner.

Bowline on a Bight

The Bowline on a Bight is an ancient Bowline variation still used
in water rescue work. It easily forms large loops in any part of the

46

Knots

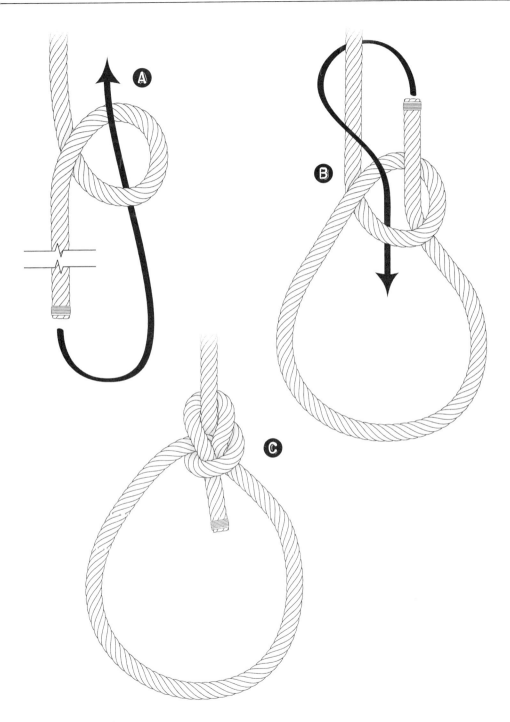

Figure 40. Bowline.

Knots, Bends, and Hitches for Mariners

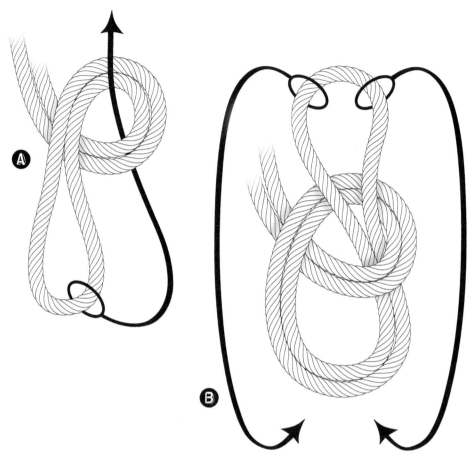

Figure 41. Bowline on a Bight.

rope without regard to the rope ends. This is especially important in dealing with an exceptionally long or heavy rope. When used in sea rescue work, a conscious person can place his legs in the appropriate loops and hold onto the double parts of the line as he is pulled out of the water. If unconscious, the victim's legs must be placed in the loops and his arms crossed in front around the double lines. Then a separate line is used to secure the wrists, starting with a Clove Hitch (pages 80–82) or Lark's Head (pages 92–93) on one wrist, running around the victim's back, and ending with a Round Turn with Two Half Hitches (pages 78–80) on the other wrist. This configuration allows all the tension to be applied to the Bowline on a Bight. The knot's only disadvantage is that the loops can slide, so tension must be applied nearly equally to both resulting loops.

Knots

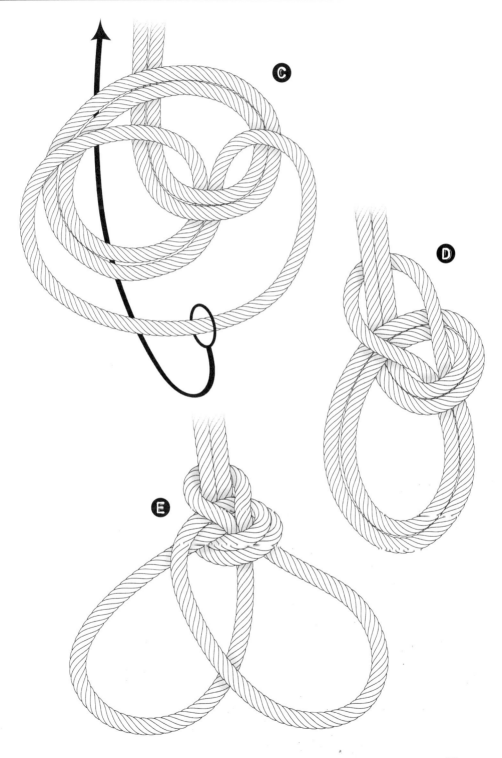

Knots, Bends, and Hitches for Mariners

To rapidly tie a Bowline on a Bight, grasp the legs of a bight and form an overhand loop with its tip to the right (Figure 41A). Next, take the bight tip and go through the overhand loop from behind (Figure 41B). Then take the bight tip down over the entire knot and up into its final position (Figure 41C). Finally, properly draw up the Bowline by pulling the two legs of the bight tight on the working part (Figure 41D) to produce the knot shown in Figure 41E.

Slipped Bowline

The Slipped Bowline is useful when the load on the loop is constant and you need a quick release. Start by tying a Bowline (Figure 42A), except make the last tuck of the knot with the end doubled in a bight (Figures 42B and 42C). Shape the knot and pull very tight in order to prevent slipping. The knot is quickly released by pulling the bitter end (Figure 42D).

Angler's Loop (Perfection Knot)

The Angler's Loop forms a strong, nonslipping, fixed loop at any position along most types of line, including bungee and shock cord. With a little practice, it is easy to tie and to remember, and it is suitable for any size of line. This knot is used primarily as a fixed loop over a spar or cleat, but it can also be used with other knots or lines, such as cinching lines. Its disadvantage is that it can be difficult to untie and may be weaker than the Bowline due to its many tight turns.

Tie the Angler's Knot by forming a small underhand loop with the tip of the loop up, and a large overhand loop with the tip of the loop down. Starting in front of the small loop leg crossing, place a turn around the original underhand loop as seen in Figure 43A.

Twist the large lower loop as shown in Figure 42B. Then lift the bottom of the large lower loop through the initial top loop from the front and shape the knot as in Figures 43C and 43D.

For added security, add a half hitch as shown in Figures 43E and 43F.

Painter's Bowline

This variation of the Bowline is used by boat painters to support a paint can. It is handy because a quick loop can be formed at any point in the middle of a line. Sailors find it excellent for securing

50

Knots

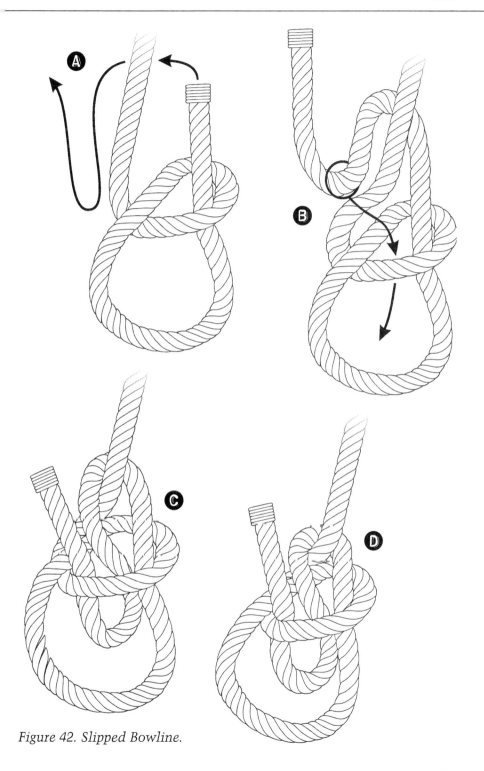

Figure 42. Slipped Bowline.

Knots, Bends, and Hitches for Mariners

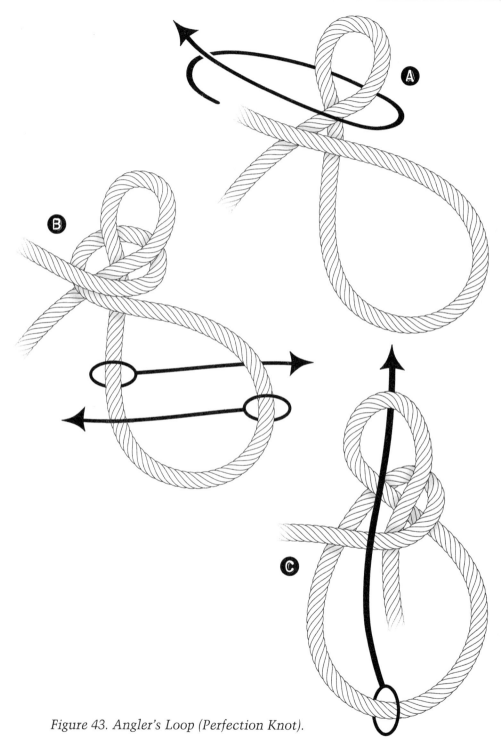

Figure 43. Angler's Loop (Perfection Knot).

Knots

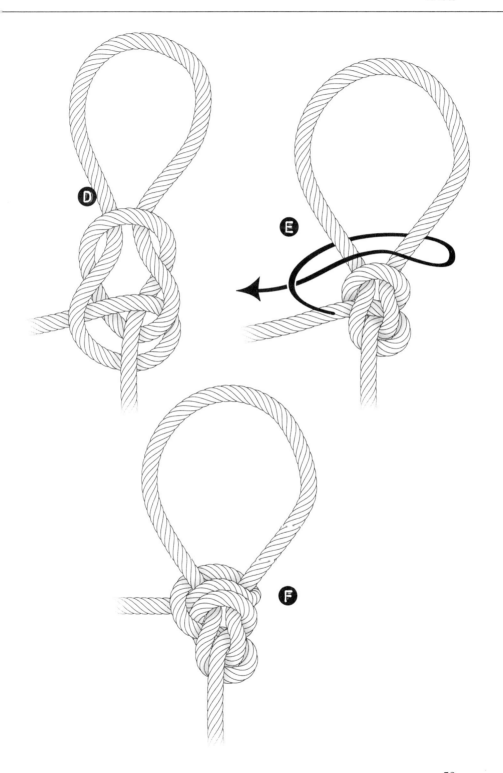

53

Knots, Bends, and Hitches for Mariners

light tackle to be carried aloft, since it is rapidly tied and easily untied.

Cast the Painter's Bowline by forming an overhand loop in a secured line. Grasp a bight of line about 2 feet below the loop and above the bitter end of the line. Go through the paint can bail (handle) with the bight, leaving the paint can bail in the lower loop as shown in Figure 44A. Next, take the bight up and behind the upper part of the secured line, then down through the original overhand loop and out past the lower formed loop holding the paint can bail (Figure 44A). Make sure the bight (X) extends far enough through the overhand loop to prevent slipping (Figure 44B).

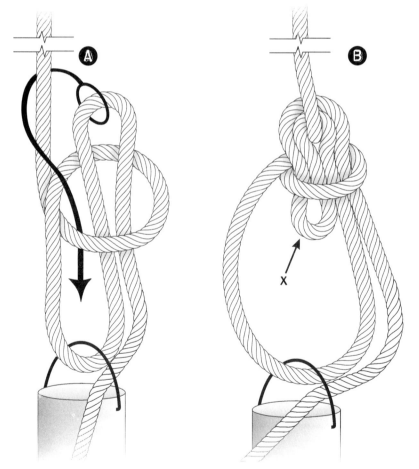

Figure 44. Painter's Bowline.

Spanish Bowline

This Bowline variant is used for water rescue and hoisting long objects in a horizontal position. Although two loops are formed, they are connected, and a greater load on one loop may cause that loop to enlarge while the other loop gets smaller. This disadvantage may be an advantage if two different-size loops are required and need to be adjusted.

Tie the Spanish Bowline in four steps, using three initial loops, as shown in Figure 45A, with the central loop much larger than the other two. Next, fold the central large loop over the side loops as in Figure 45B. Then simultaneously pull the lateral edges of the large loop through the two small loops as in Figure 45C. Hold these two loops and pull the working parts of the rope to form the knot shown in Figure 45D.

This knot is frequently a feature on demonstration boards because of its beauty and apparent complexity.

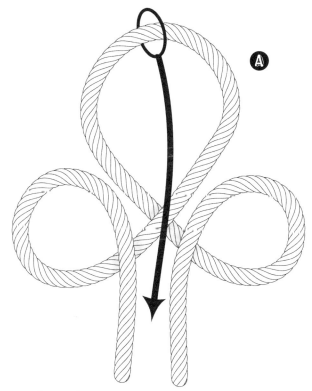

Figure 45. Spanish Bowline.

Knots, Bends, and Hitches for Mariners

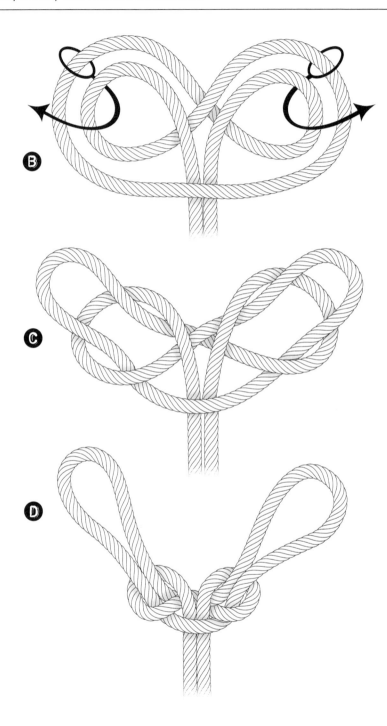

Figure 45 (continued). Spanish Bowline.

Japanese Bowline

The Japanese Bowline is primarily a decorative knot, always seeming to find a place on demonstration knot boards or in Bowline discussions. It forms two adjustable loops, and if the load is equally distributed between both loops opposing the two support-

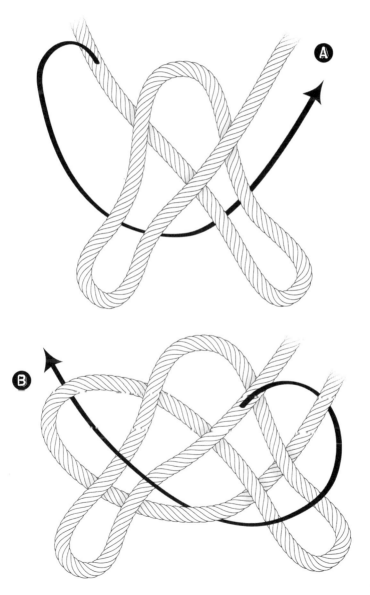

Figure 46. Japanese Bowline.

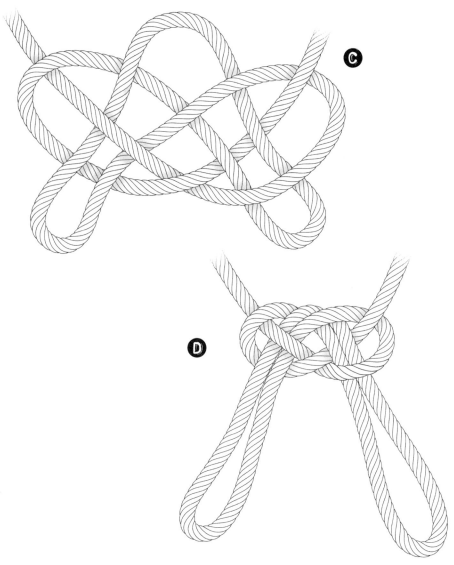

Figure 46 (continued). Japanese Bowline.

ing strands, it has some practical use. Remember that reducing the load on one loop will cause slipping.

Tie the Japanese Bowline by starting with a pretzel configuration of loops as in Figure 46A. Then, cross the working part under the two loops, as shown by the arrow. Next, cross the bitter end to the opposite side, following the arrow in Figure 46B.

Using two fingers of one hand, one through each loop, simultaneously pull on the working part and the bitter end as shown in Figure 46C. When the Japanese Bowline is correctly tied, it will look like the knot in Figure 46D.

Three-Part Crown Knot

The Three-Part Crown Knot forms two secure, nonadjustable loops. It is a handsome knot, easy to make, and good for decorative purposes. It is used infrequently by mariners because of the difficulty in predetermining the size of the loops. The strain must be on both sides of the line, or the working part can be seized to the bitter end after the two loops are formed.

To tie a Three-Part Crown Knot, first form two loops by folding back the end of a bight. Next, hold the bight closed, and move the bitter end and the working part together between the two ini-

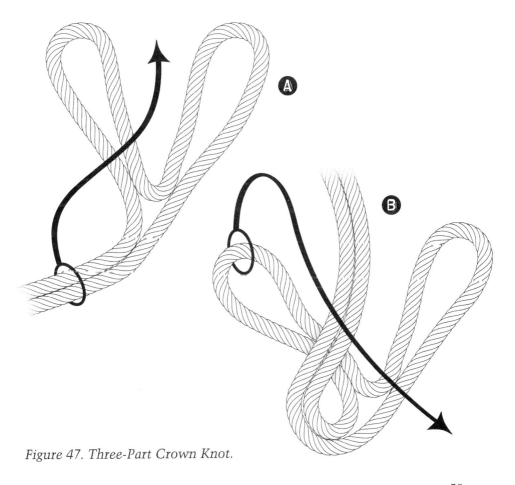

Figure 47. Three-Part Crown Knot.

Knots, Bends, and Hitches for Mariners

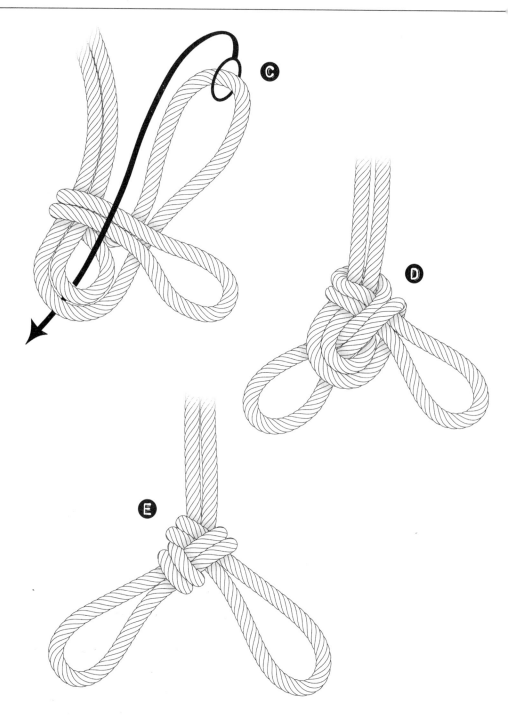

Figure 47 (continued). Three-Part Crown Knot.

tial loops and over one loop (Figure 47A). Then, fold that loop up and over the intersection (Figure 47B). Next, pull the other loop down and through the hole (Figures 47C and 47D). Finish by gradually tightening the knot by pulling on the loops (Figure 47E).

True Lover's Knot (Clover Knot or Cross Knot)

A True Lover's Knot has three loops at right angles to one another. It is stable only if the load is equally distributed on all three loops and the working part and bitter end together lead away in the fourth direction. Other than its intrinsic beauty, this knot has few redeeming features—you probably truly love knots if you use it at all. (Maybe this is how it got its name.)

To tie the knot, start with an Overhand Knot, as shown in Figure 48A. Following the arrow in Figure 48A, start a second Overhand Knot, linked to the first, and complete it following the arrow in Figure 48B. Figure 48C shows how the intermediate configuration should appear before proceeding. Following the arrows in Figures 48C and 48D, carefully pull out the three loops from

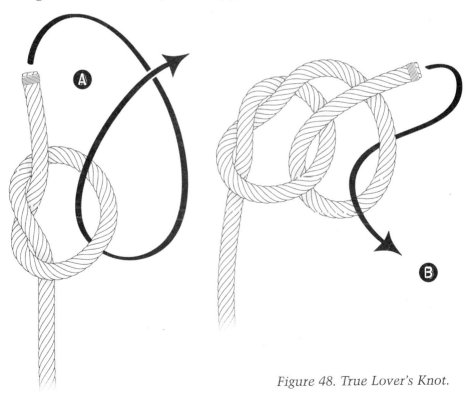

Figure 48. True Lover's Knot.

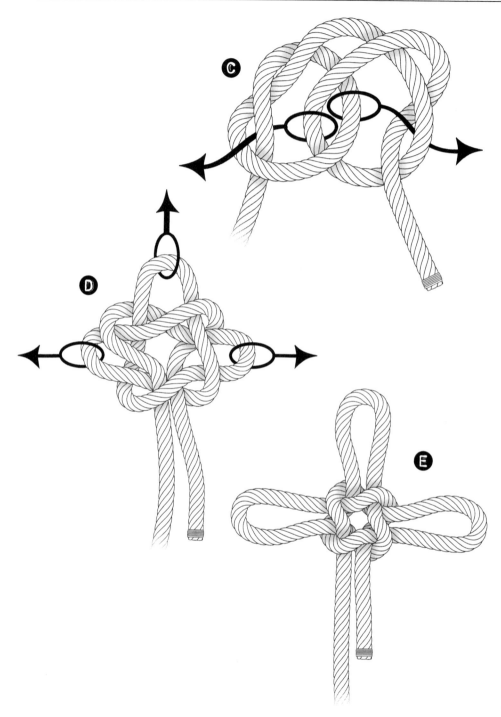

Figure 48 (continued). True Lover's Knot.

inside the knot while holding the working part and the bitter end together. Finally, adjust the knot by pulling the three loops and the working part/bitter end, each in their own direction from the center of the knot, to achieve the result shown in Figure 48E.

Japanese Success Knot

The Japanese Success Knot derives its name from its final configuration as a cross on one side (Figure 49E) and a rough square on the other (Figure 49F). This forms the Japanese word *kanau*, which means "the desire realized." The knot is useful as a firm loop and is included here because of its symmetrical beauty.

Cast the Japanese Success Knot by forming an overhand loop (Figure 49A) with the tip of the loop up. Grasp a bight from the working part and place it over the bitter end. Take the bitter end up and over the bight and down through the original overhand loop and back up through the bight (Figure 49B). Then, begin to draw up and tighten the knot by pulling in the direction of the arrows in Figures 49C and 49D. After tightening, the configuration will appear as the knot in Figure 49E.

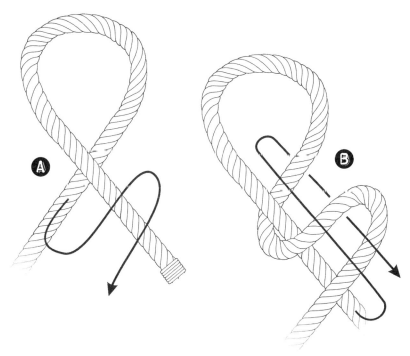

Figure 49. Japanese Success Knot.

Knots, Bends, and Hitches for Mariners

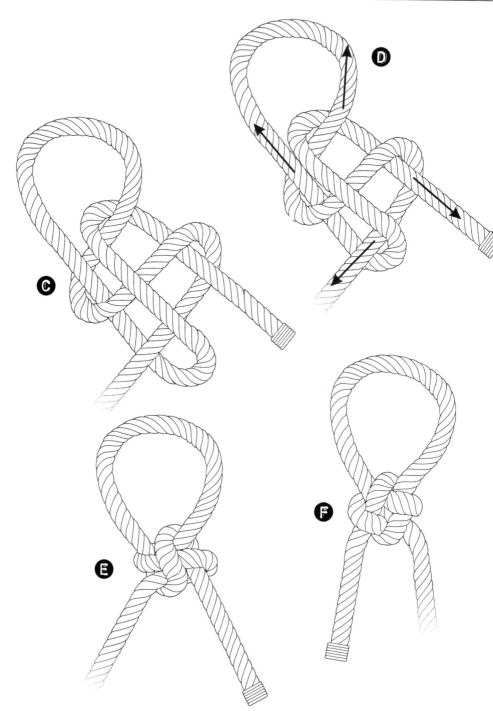

Figure 49 (continued). Japanese Success Knot.

64

Jury Mast Knot

The Jury Mast Knot is an emergency knot, such as for supporting a jury-rigged mast on a dismasted sailboat. Begin the Jury Mast Knot by making three underhand loops, each going under the one before (Figures 50A and 50B). Follow the arrows in Figure 50C and pull the inner bights of the outer loops to the side while extending the upper bight of the inner loop to form the knot. Tighten the knot to look like Figure 50D. Pull the rope ends aside as shown in Figure 50D so they can be seized to the side loops as shown in Figure 50E.

Temporarily screw or nail wood blocks to the jury mast under the knot to keep the knot from slipping down the mast. You may also use a Constrictor Knot (pages 100, 102–3) if blocks are not available.

Finally, to support the jury mast, bend the stays and shrouds to the three loops with Double Sheet Bends (pages 70, 71).

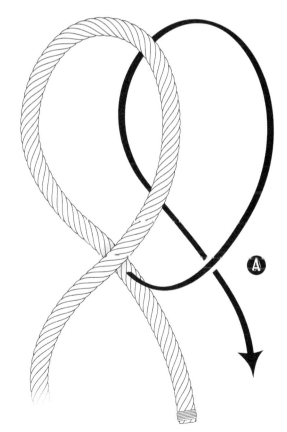

Figure 50. Jury Mast Knot.

Knots, Bends, and Hitches for Mariners

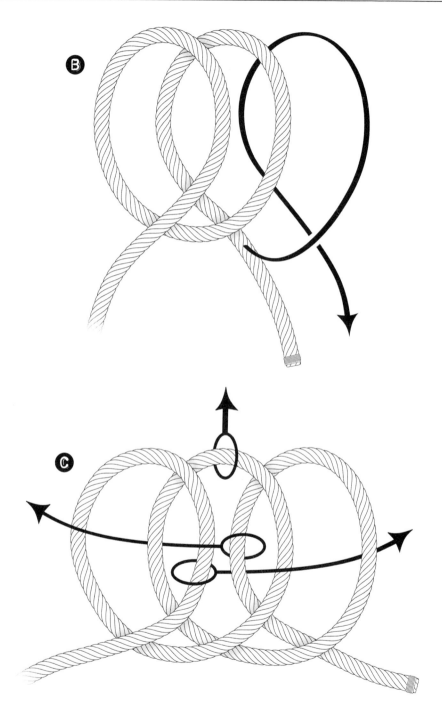

Figure 50 (continued). Jury Mast Knot.

Knots

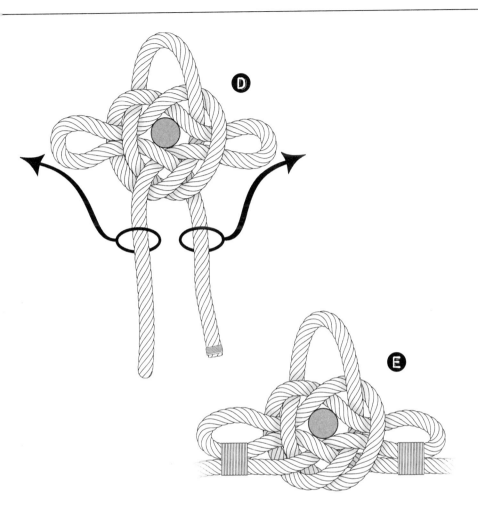

5

Bends

Bends are knots that fasten two lines together. Sailors talk of "bending one line to another." The first five bends presented here are all widely respected in the marine world for function and safety. The last knot, the Square or Reef Knot, is included because it is so well known. Unfortunately, whatever good reputation it has is certainly undeserved. It should never be used to join lines that will be under load. Look to the first five bends instead. The Square Knot is fine for reefing sails, tying shoelaces, and tying packages for shipping.

Sheet Bend

The Sheet Bend is the fastest and probably the best method of joining two lines, especially if the lines are of unequal diameter. It is unlikely to capsize even with a sudden load. The greater the load on this knot, the better the jamming action. An example of its use would be in towing. If one line already has an Eye Splice (pages 116–22), the knot is halfway cast. This variation will be covered on pages 70 and 72 as a Becket Bend. It is easily converted to a Double Sheet Bend (less likely to slip when using braided line; pages 70, 71). If the knot is used to extend an anchor rode, the bitter ends should be seized to the working parts.

Bends

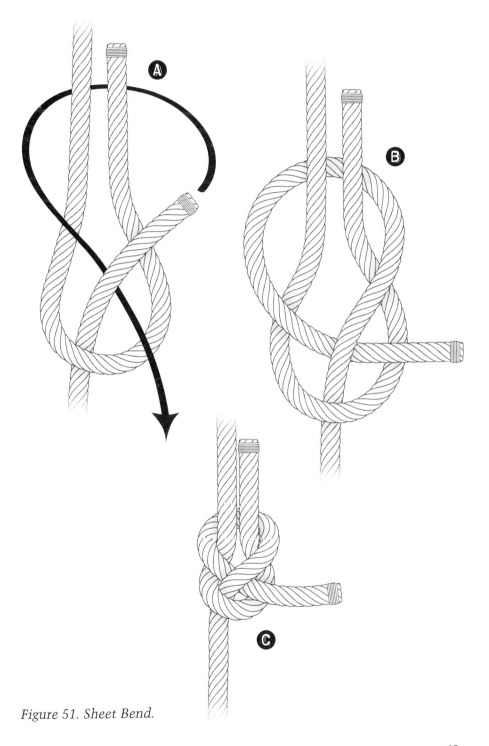

Figure 51. Sheet Bend.

Knots, Bends, and Hitches for Mariners

Tie the Sheet Bend by forming an open bight in the first line (Figure 51A). Thread the second line up through the loop (Figure 51B), around the back of the loop, and back under itself. Take care to ensure that both bitter ends are on the same side of the knot and not diagonally opposite. Pull and shape the knot before permitting a load to be applied (Figure 51C).

Double Sheet Bend

When joining slick, thick, or stiff ropes or lines, the Double Sheet Bend is recommended. Doubling the turns on the knot makes it more resistant to slipping and provides extra holding power. This is especially true when the lines are exposed to the effects of wave action and water.

The Double Sheet Bend shown in Figure 52C begins in the same manner as the single Sheet Bend as shown in Figure 51A; that is, with an open bight in the first line. Then, pass the end of the second line up through the loop and twice around the legs of the loop as shown in Figures 52A and 52B. The same caution against diagonal bitter ends (see Sheet Bend above) applies. Another word of caution: When drawing up this knot, you cannot simply pull the ends to tighten the knot. You must carefully work out the slack in the turns before finally pulling the legs of the open bight tight as traction against the other working part.

The finished Double Sheet Bend is shown in Figure 51C. If the knot is relatively permanent, you may seize the legs of the open bight as well as the other working part to the other bitter end.

Becket Bend (Becket Hitch)

A common boating situation is the need to make two short dock lines into one longer one. The most efficient way to do this is to use a Becket Bend. An Eye Splice (pages 116–22) in the end of one dock line is the bight for the Becket Bend. Complete the Becket Bend by threading the other line up through the eye (Figure 53), around the back of the eye, and back under itself, the same as you would for the Sheet Bend.

Use this same procedure to attach a line to a metal hook, in which case it is called a Becket Hitch; the hook is the bight.

70

Bends

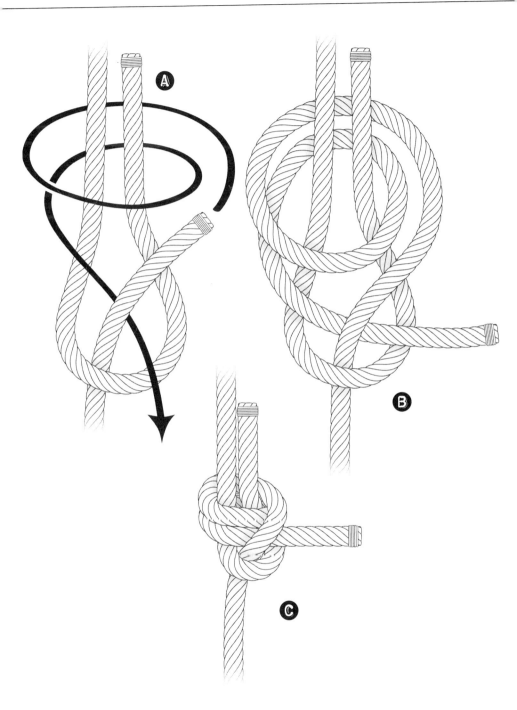

Figure 52. Double Sheet Bend.

Knots, Bends, and Hitches for Mariners

Figure 53. Becket Bend.

Carrick Bend

The Carrick Bend has been praised by some as the nearest thing to a perfect bend. Wet or dry, it will not slip. It is easy to untie and can't jam. The only detraction is that it is a little tricky to tie, and there are a number of incorrect but similar versions. The Carrick Bend is especially useful when bending large lines or *hawsers* together.

Cast this knot on a table or other flat surface. Begin the Carrick Bend by placing an underhand loop in the end of line 1 on the table (Figure 54A). Lay the bitter end of line 2 under the first loop, with the working parts on opposite sides of the knot (Figure 54B). Cross bitter end 2 over working part 1, then under bitter end 1 (Figure 54C), then over the near side of the loop, then under working part 2, and finally over the far side of the loop (Figure 54D). The result is another underhand loop in line 2 that is woven into the

Bends

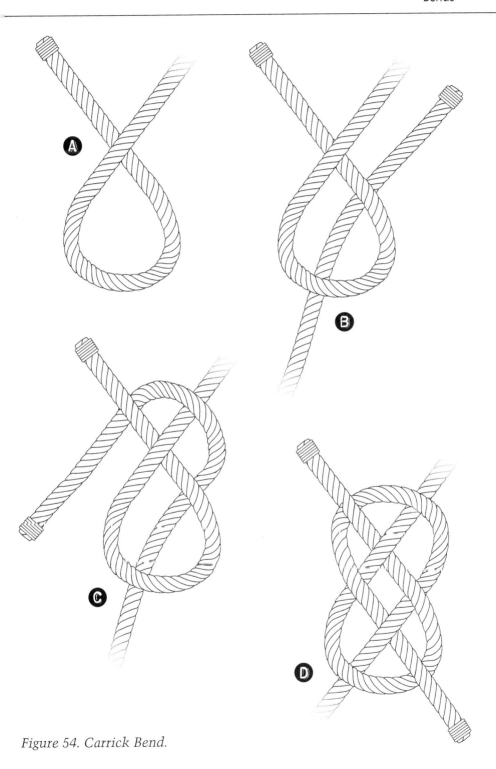

Figure 54. Carrick Bend.

Knots, Bends, and Hitches for Mariners

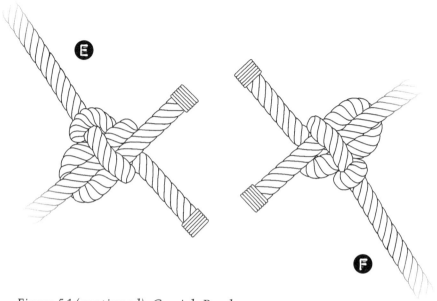

Figure 54 (continued). Carrick Bend.

underhand loop in line 1. Two conditions are critical when viewing the knot before tightening it. One, the bitter ends are diagonally opposite in the knot as are the two working parts. Two, every crossing in the knot of every part of line follows an over-under-over-under path. Both are shown clearly in Figure 54D. No part of line in the knot crosses two adjacent other parts. After pulling the knot tight, everything changes. You won't recognize the result (Figures 54E and 54F). This is why it is so important to get the crossings right before tightening the knot.

Hawser Bend

As previously demonstrated, the Sheet Bend is useful for joining two ropes of unequal size. The Hawser Bend complements this concept and is especially helpful when joining a light line to a very heavy line. This bend is frequently used when it is necessary to join a heavy line (towing hawser) on a large ship with a lighter towing line on a smaller vessel.

Always make the bight in the thicker line. Then pass the bitter end of the lighter line under the loop and weave it, much like a shoelace, four or five times as seen in Figure 55A. End the knot

Bends

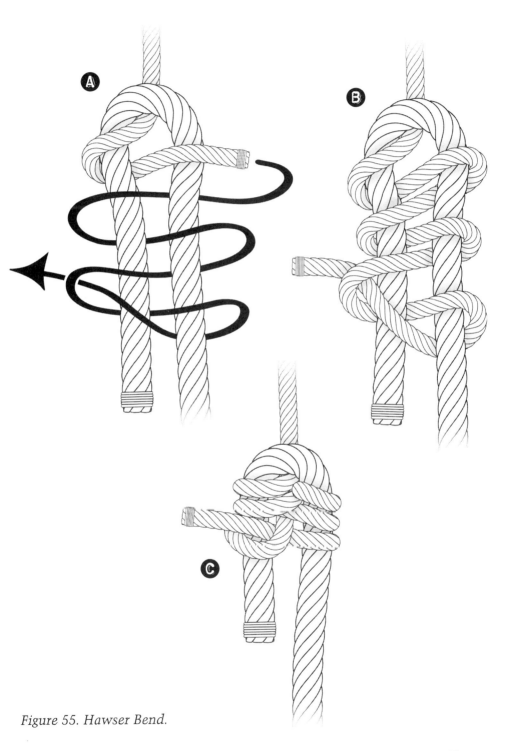

Figure 55. Hawser Bend.

Knots, Bends, and Hitches for Mariners

with a half hitch (Figure 55B). Finally, shape and tighten it (Figure 55C) to prevent capsizing when the load is applied.

Although you may never use this bend, it is worth knowing because it is easy to learn, and once you know it, you will always have it in your knot repertoire.

Reef (Square) Knot

Use the Reef Knot only in low-stress, noncritical situations. It will easily capsize. Used properly, the Reef Knot will bind something such as a reefed sail. Another disadvantage of the Reef

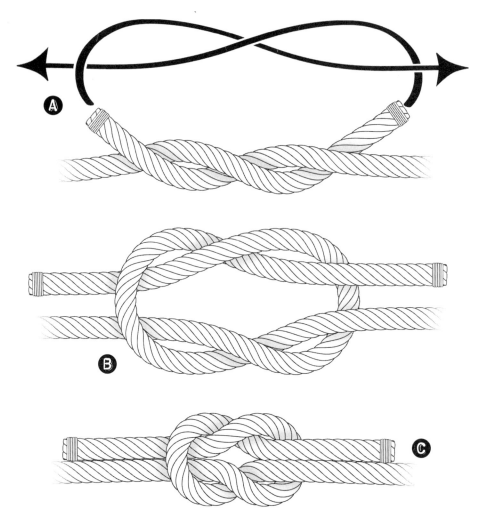

Figure 56. Reef (Square) Knot.

Bends

Knot is that it may be hard to untie when it has been under tension or is wet.

There are several methods of casting the Reef Knot. The one shown in Figures 56A and 56B needs no text description. Another method is to form an open bight in the end of the first line, such as the left line in Figure 56B. Complete the knot by casting a bight in the second line end and weaving it through and around the bight in the first line as shown in Figure 56B. Make sure both bitter ends are on the same side of the knot as shown in the illustrations. Finally, pull it tight, as in Figure 56C.

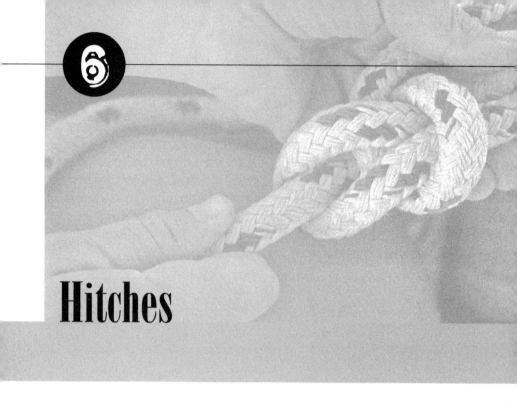

Hitches

Hitches are divided into two categories—attaching hitches and gathering hitches. Attaching hitches are used to secure a rope—either the rope end or a bight—to a hook, ring, spar, or anchor. Gathering hitches are used to form a loop or noose in a rope to gather loose items into a bundle.

Attaching Hitches

Round Turn with Two Half Hitches

The Round Turn with Two Half Hitches is another basic mariner's knot. It is simple to tie, easy to learn, and holds fast in most situations. Use it as a temporary method of fastening a line to another object such as a spar, ring, or bitt, or even in the central hole of a hollow-base cleat. Note that the round turn starting this knot is better than a simple turn due to its ability to resist slipping and to distribute the contact with the spar or ring over two turns rather than one, thus reducing abrasion and stress on the rope.

To begin, take two complete turns around a spar or ring as in Figure 57A. Next, apply two half hitches on the working part, as in Figures 57B and 57C. Then, slip the knot tightly against the ob-

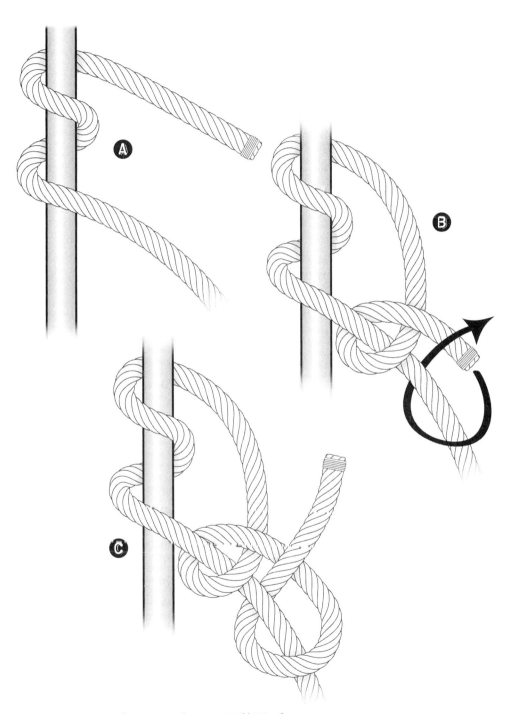

Figure 57. Round Turn with Two Half Hitches.

Knots, Bends, and Hitches for Mariners

ject. For a more permanent application, you may seize the bitter end against the working part.

Clove Hitch (for tall piles)

The Clove Hitch is a special knot with some peculiarities. It is used to attach a line to a round pile. On the plus side, it is a tenacious slip knot that will tightly constrict a wood pile and not slip down, even if the pile is tapered from large-on-top to small-at-the-bottom. Also, it is easy to tie and untie under a strain. The bad characteristic of a Clove Hitch is that if the load moves back and forth, the knot will rotate on the pile, allowing the working part to pull out of the knot and the bitter end to be drawn into the knot. Eventually, the bitter end will disappear and so will the knot. However, this is easily countered by adding two half hitches with the bitter end around the working part, as described in the instructions.

At this point, you may be wondering, with almost 4,000 knots available to choose from, why select a knot that needs another knot to secure it? The answer is that the Clove Hitch's good properties are somewhat unique, and the "crutch" (the two half hitches) is really just another Clove Hitch around the working part of the line. Practice tying the Clove Hitch around a vertical cylindrical object.

Start with a bitter end long enough to wrap twice around the post and still have 2 feet of line left over for the half hitches. Wrap the bitter end around the post, and when you come back to the working part, pass under the working part and immediately cross over the wrap you have just made so the next wrap will be on top of the first (Figure 58A). Make a second wrap in the same direction as the first, and when you come to the crossing, pass the bitter end under the crossing and pull it tight (Figure 58B). On the back side of the knot, the two wraps should be parallel and tight. On the front side of the knot, the crossing should go from the bottom turn across both the bitter end and the working part to the top turn (Figure 58C).

Next make two half hitches as in Figures 57B and 57C (Round Turn with Two Half Hitches) with the remaining bitter end. Pass the bitter end **over** and around the working part and back up around the working part and between the bitter end and the Clove Hitch. Draw it tight. The bitter end should now be

80

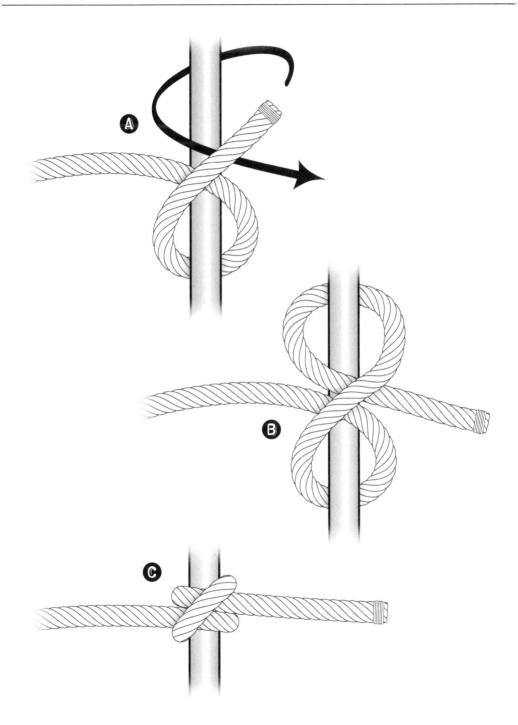

Figure 58. Clove Hitch for a tall pile.

Knots, Bends, and Hitches for Mariners

trapped between itself and the Clove Hitch. This is the first half hitch. For the second half hitch, pass the bitter end **over** and around the working part in the same direction. When you come to the crossing, pass the bitter end under the crossing and pull it tight. This is the second half hitch. The construction sounds like the Clove Hitch, and the final knot looks like a small Clove Hitch.

Clove Hitch (for short piles)

When you can slip a line over a bollard or pile, use this simpler and more rapid method of tying a Clove Hitch. Begin by forming two underhand loops side by side, each large enough to enclose the pile (Figure 59A). Then slide the second loop over the first loop as in Figures 59B and 59C. Place the two loops over the pile and pull on the working part and the bitter end to tighten the knot. Add two half hitches as described above to secure the knot.

Cleat Hitch

The Cleat Hitch is another special knot. Besides being secure and reliable, its other important trait is that it can be untied under load. It is used to secure a line to a cleat. The Cleat Hitch consists of turns around the base of a cleat followed by a figure-eight weave around the horns of the cleat.

If the cleat surface is rough or sharp edged, then a 540° round turn might suffice before adding the top weave (Figure 60A). But many of the cleats today are smooth and polished with round bases, requiring you to wrap the line three full times around the base to make it secure.

In either case, the final weave is performed with the bitter end coming out from under one cleat horn, across the top of the cleat diagonally and under the other cleat horn, then back diagonally and over the first diagonal line (Figure 60B). Continue under the first horn and around and back diagonally and under the second diagonal (Figure 60C). The first and third diagonals should be parallel and under the second diagonal.

Anchor Bend (a Hitch)

The Anchor Bend is a variation of the Round Turn with Two Half Hitches (pages 78–80). It is also a slip knot but is more secure, and

Hitches

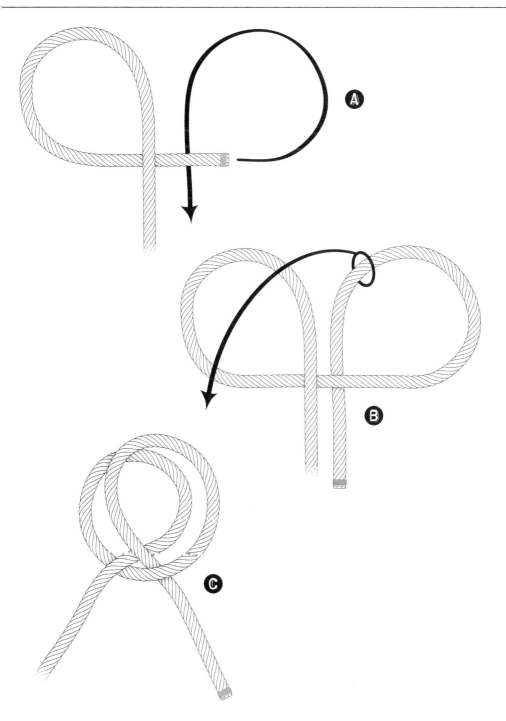

Figure 59. Clove Hitch for a short pile.

Knots, Bends, and Hitches for Mariners

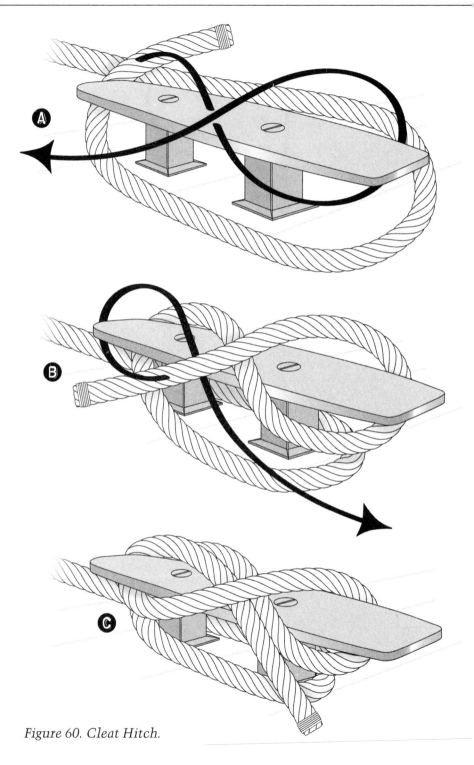

Figure 60. Cleat Hitch.

Hitches

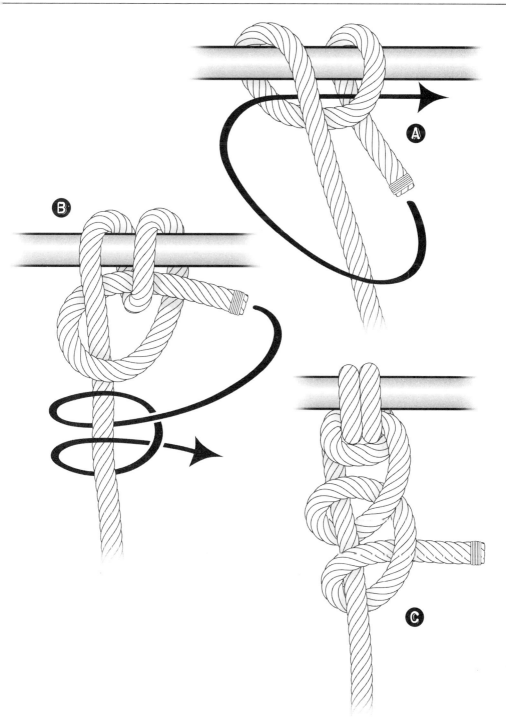

Figure 61. Anchor Bend (plus two half hitches for security).

when fastened to the ring on an anchor shank, tends to bind to the ring tightly enough to keep the knot from rotating around the ring under load. This is good when you consider that there may well be abrasive material surrounding the ring and the knot, and the knot is underwater where you can't see wear that might be occurring.

Start with a conventional round turn around the anchor ring (Figure 61A). Then, pass the bitter end over the working part and between the round turn and the ring. Pull it tight with the bitter end (Figure 61B), and then finish the knot with two half hitches, as shown by the arrow in Figure 61B and in Figure 61C. For added security, seize the bitter end to the working part. Leave some slack in the bitter end before seizing so the rest of the knot can slide along the working part and bind effectively on the anchor ring.

Rolling Hitch

The Rolling Hitch is used to secure one line to another line or to a smooth cylindrical object, such as a post floating in the water. Use this hitch when you want the knot to grip the object and not slip lengthwise along it. Besides the usual qualities of a good knot,

Figure 62. Rolling Hitch.

Hitches

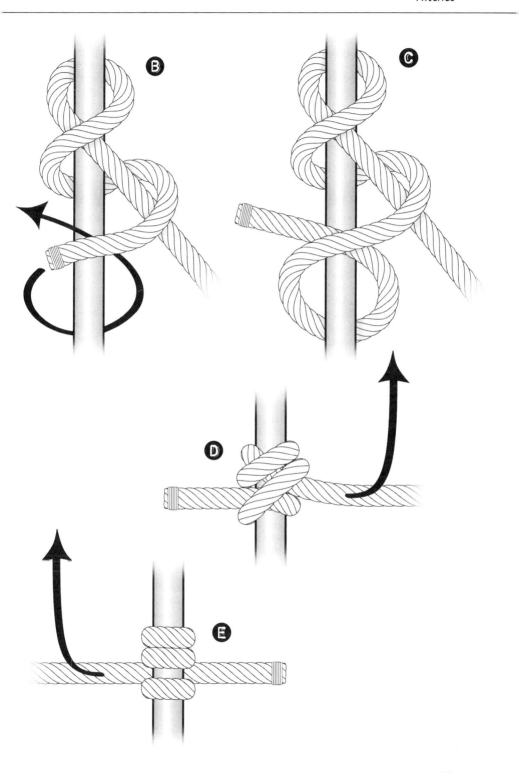

Knots, Bends, and Hitches for Mariners

the Rolling Hitch can be tied with one hand while you hold the object you are tying it to with the other hand.

Hold the object in your left hand. With the working part of the line running opposite to the direction you will be hauling the object, wrap the bitter end around the object with your right hand (Figure 62A). When you come to the working part at the end of the first wrap, cross over the working part and add a second wrap, again crossing over the working part (Figure 62B).

Wrap another turn, and when you again come to the working part, slip the bitter end under the last wrap just before crossing the working part (Figure 62C). Pull the wraps tight. Now pull the working part back in the opposite direction and over the knot. You are ready to use the rolling hitch to haul or drag the object (Figures 62D and 62E).

Buntline Hitch

When you need a simple knot that will hold under a load, think of the Buntline Hitch. The Buntline Hitch can be rapidly and easily passed through a ring or around a bar or spar. By splitting its back, it can be loosened easily. You can use it for attaching a genoa sheet to the clew of a sail or a halyard to a shackle.

To tie the Buntline Hitch, take the bitter end behind and out through a ring as in Figure 63A. Come to the right of the working part to form a U around the working part, holding it in place with your index finger and thumb.

Next, bring the bitter end around and in front of the working part, behind the right limb of the loop, and down through the newly formed loop (Figure 63B).

Shape the knot, making sure it is a tight Clove Hitch (pages 80–82) on the working part, then cinch down tightly as in Figures 63C and 63D. The hitch will slide up toward the ring and tighten on the ring.

Slipped Buntline Hitch

The Slipped Buntline Hitch is somewhat more difficult to tie, but worth learning because it is easy to untie.

To cast this knot, prepare an overhand loop, holding it in place with your thumb and forefinger as described for the Buntline Hitch above and shown in Figure 64A.

Hitches

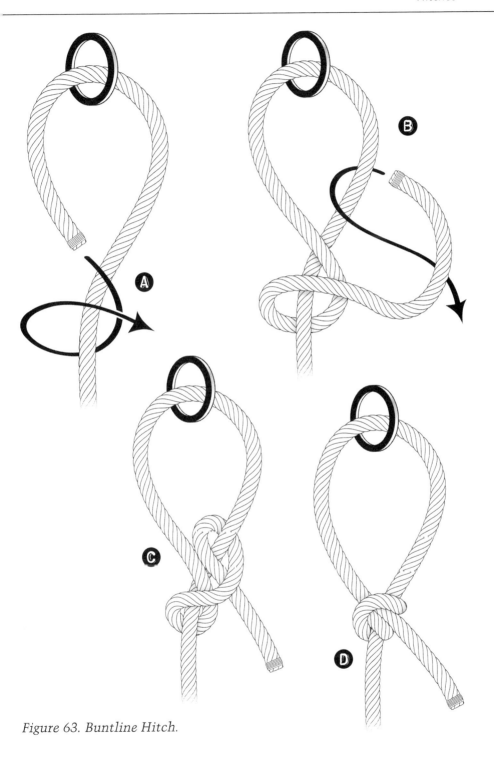

Figure 63. Buntline Hitch.

Knots, Bends, and Hitches for Mariners

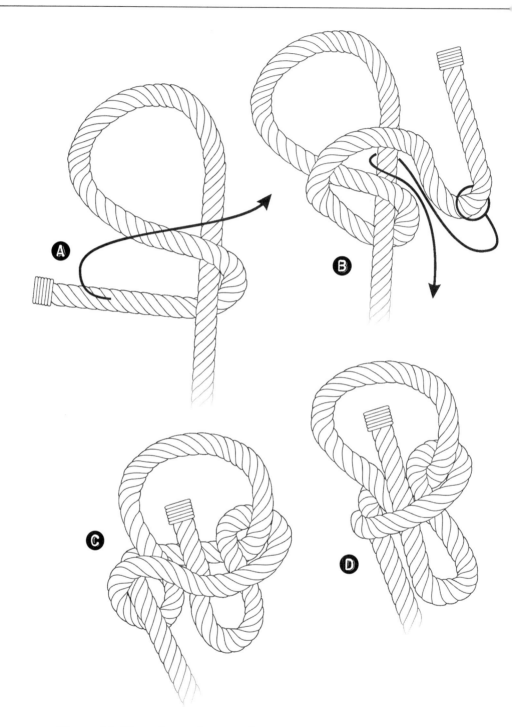

Figure 64. Slipped Buntline Hitch.

Hitches

Take a bight in the bitter end, around the right leg of the loop, and back under the working part (Figure 64B). Then, tighten the knot by pulling on the two loops (Figure 64C) while still holding the working part as shown in Figure 64D.

Tugboat Hitch (Bitt Hitch)

Towing or being towed is a special situation on a boat with many safety considerations. The Tugboat Hitch is the special knot to use to secure the ends of the tow line to the boats. It holds well,

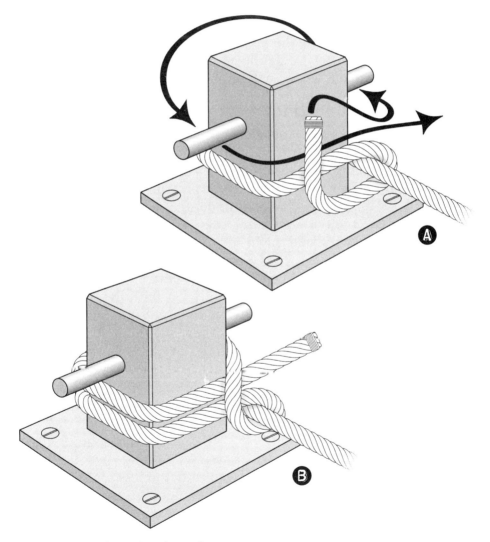

Figure 65. Tugboat (Bitt) Hitch.

Knots, Bends, and Hitches for Mariners

won't jam, and can be untied or released under load in an emergency. Make sure before you tow or are towed that the deck hardware on both boats is designed for towing. This means through-bolted cleats or frame-mounted samson posts. Also, it is extremely dangerous to use line that stretches, such as laid nylon, for towing. Polypropylene or polyethylene rope is best for towing because of its low elasticity. People have been injured or killed in towing operations when a stretchy line parted or a cleat came loose.

To apply a Bitt Hitch, take the bitter end around the base to the left and lead the end over and around the working part (Figure 65A). Finish by leading the bitter end around the back of the bitt, ending in a half hitch under the norman pin as shown in Figure 65B. You can add a second half hitch for security.

Lark's Head (Cow Hitch)

About 2,000 years ago, a physician used the Lark's Head to produce a sling for the treatment of broken bones. Today this knot survives to secure such things as baggage tags. It is not used much aboard ship unless both the bitter end and the working part are under tension. If only one part is under tension, the knot slips. There are two methods of casting this hitch: the Lark's Head shown in Figure 66B and the Inside Cow Hitch shown in Figure 67C on page 94.

The Lark's Head version of the Cow Hitch begins with an underhand loop followed by an overhand loop, with the tip of each loop up (Figure 66A). Hold the line with both hands and fold the loops together, like closing a book. Then, slip them over the open end of the spar (Figure 66B) and pull the two ends down through the loops.

If the loops can't be slipped over the end of the spar, take the bitter end of the line over the spar, go around and in back of the working part, back over the spar, and back down through the bight parallel to the working part. To accomplish the same end, the Lark's Head can be toggled (pages 145, 147–48).

The problem with a Lark's Head is that unless tension is applied to both working ends equally, the knot slips toward the end with more tension. To offset this tendency, another version of the Cow Hitch may be used. This is the Inside Cow Hitch described next.

92

Hitches

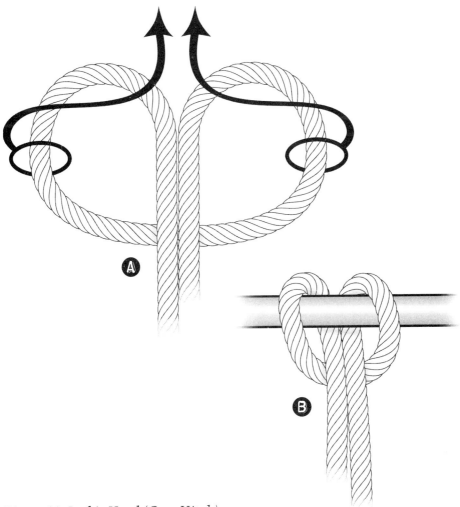

Figure 66. Lark's Head (Cow Hitch).

Inside Cow Hitch

This knot serves the same purpose as a Lark's Head, except it cin-ches tightly to the ring or spar rather than being prone to slipping.

Start the Inside Cow Hitch with the same sequence as the Lark's Head. Make two loops—an overhand loop followed by an underhand loop—and place this combination flat under the spar or ring. Bring the two working parts of the rope down around the spar and through their respective loops as in Figure 67A. Then pull down on the two working parts as in Figure 67B. Continue

Knots, Bends, and Hitches for Mariners

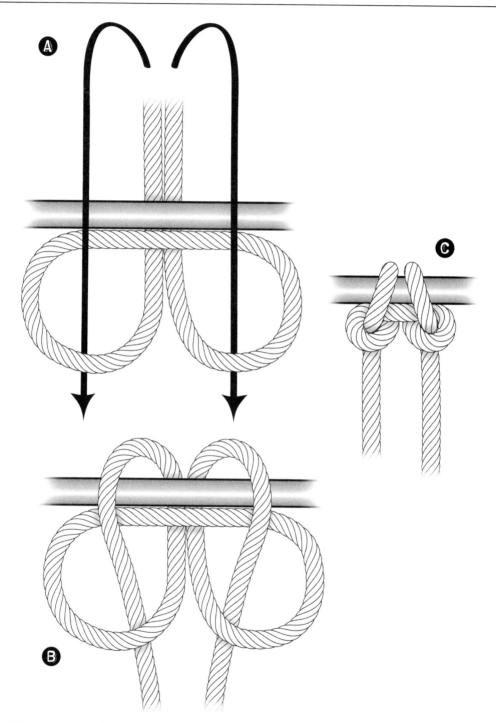

Figure 67. Inside Cow Hitch.

pulling downward on the working parts to tighten the hitch around the spar. Tighten and shape the knot as in Figure 67C.

When the Inside Cow Hitch is tightened securely, it rarely slips, and even this possibility can be avoided by adding a stopper knot to one of the rope ends and using the other as the working part.

Jar Sling

The Jar Sling or Jug Sling Knot is a handy way to carry a bulky object, such as a water jug. The final result of this knot is an interlaced constricting knot that tightens further when pulled from both sides.

There are many published methods of casting this knot, but the simplest is the one shown here. This knot is usually made using a short piece of rope. For these tying instructions, assume there are two bitter ends. Form a closed underhand loop and take the left bitter end back and through the loop as in Figure 68A. Next, take the other bitter end and go in front of the first bitter end, back and through the loop, and down behind the new lower loop as shown in Figure 68B. Then, as shown in Figure 68C, place the right middle loop through the left middle loop. Now, taking the large upper loop, place it through the remaining loop as shown in Figure 68D.

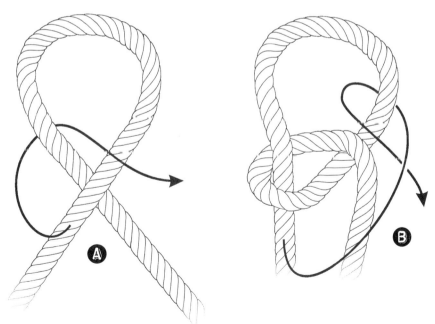

Figure 68. Jar Sling.

Knots, Bends, and Hitches for Mariners

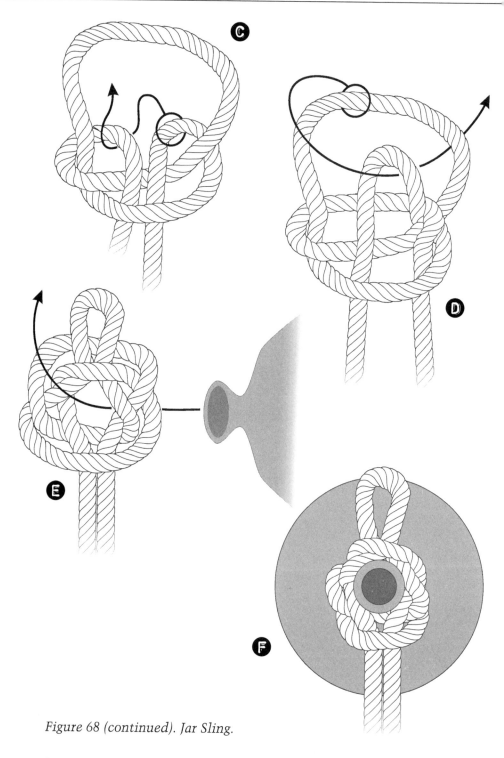

Figure 68 (continued). Jar Sling.

Shape the knot by opening the hole in the center. Place the neck of the jar in this opening (Figures 68E and 68F). Tighten the knot by pulling the two bitter ends together against the remaining loop.

Gathering Hitches
Binder's Loop
Farmers used the Binder's Loop in light line to bind a sheaf of straw, a handful of straw wisps, or a bale of hay. It can be used to bind any bundle of loose items. It is finished with two half hitches.

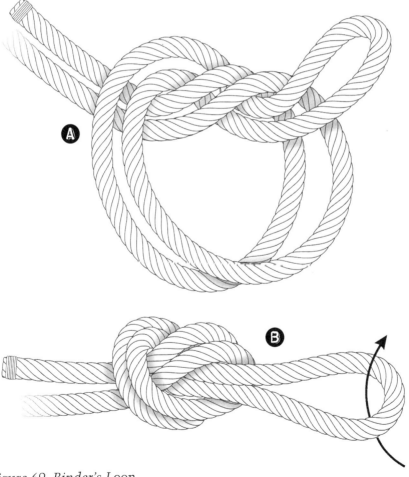

Figure 69. Binder's Loop.

Knots, Bends, and Hitches for Mariners

To tie the Binder's Loop, form a tight bight in the end of the line. Then tie an Overhand Knot below the tip of the bight (Figures 69A and 69B). Wrap the other end of the line around the bundle to bind it. Insert the end of the line through the loop (at the arrow) and pull tight. Then, tie two half hitches around the binding line to secure the knot.

Sack Knot (Twice-Turned)

The Sack Knot is a generic name given to a number of knots, such as the Bag Knot, the Miller's Knot, the Constrictor Knot, and even the Clove Hitch.

To tie a Sack Knot, take a round turn around the object to be tied (Figure 70A). Go over the working part and under both turns with the bitter end. Pull very tight and heat-melt the ends to make the knot permanent (Figure 70B).

This variation of the Sack Knot is used to secure the ends of nylon line before tying other knots, such as a Tack Knot (pages 130, 132, 133–34) or a Star Knot (pages 132, 135–39). The Sack Knot is ideal for this purpose because it is easy to apply and will not slip while you are preparing to do the heat-melt. Eventually, it is hidden in the base of the knot.

Sack Knot (Thrice-Turned)

This variation of the Sack Knot accomplishes the same objective as the Twice-Turned Sack Knot, except that it is slightly more secure.

To tie this knot, take three turns around the object. Then take the bitter end around to the left and under all three turns, as shown in Figure 71A. With pliers, pull both ends of the knot tight (Figure 71B). For permanent applications, heat-melt the ends to the knot itself.

Strangle Knot

The Strangle Knot is very effective when used to secure a group of lines.

To tie the Strangle Knot, start with a jam turn over the group of lines to be bound (Figure 72A). Continue with two more turns over the working part (Figure 72B). End with the bitter end going under the first two turns and parallel to the work-

Hitches

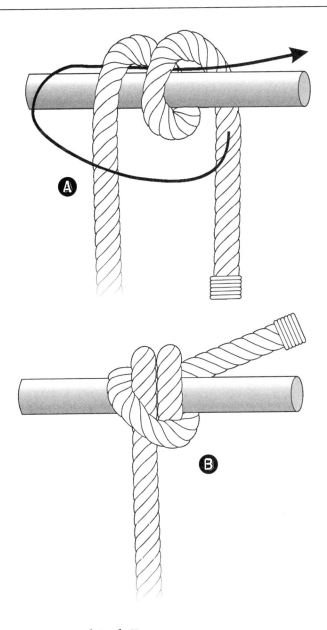

Figure 70. Twice-Turned Sack Knot.

ing part, but going in the opposite direction (Figure 72C). Use pliers to draw it up tight, then heat-melt the ends (Figure 72D). This binding knot holds exceedingly well and is a good substitute for whipping or seizing as it is faster to accomplish.

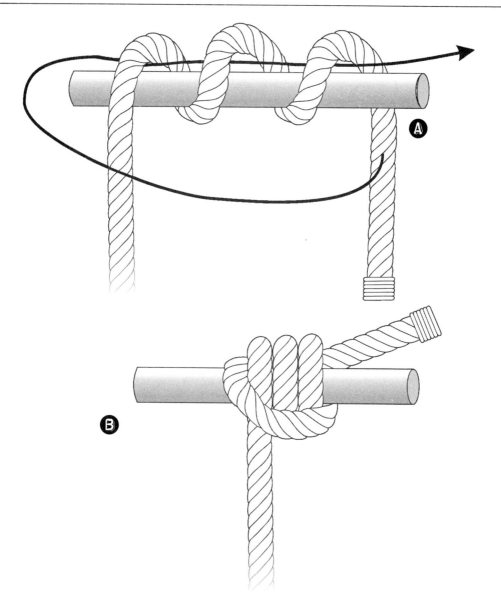

Figure 71. Thrice-Turned Sack Knot.

Constrictor Knot

The Constrictor Knot is easy to cast and is frequently used to produce a secure binding for closing a sack or to fasten a line to another line for in-line pulling (Figure 73D). Because the knot is difficult to untie, only use it in situations where you desire a

Hitches

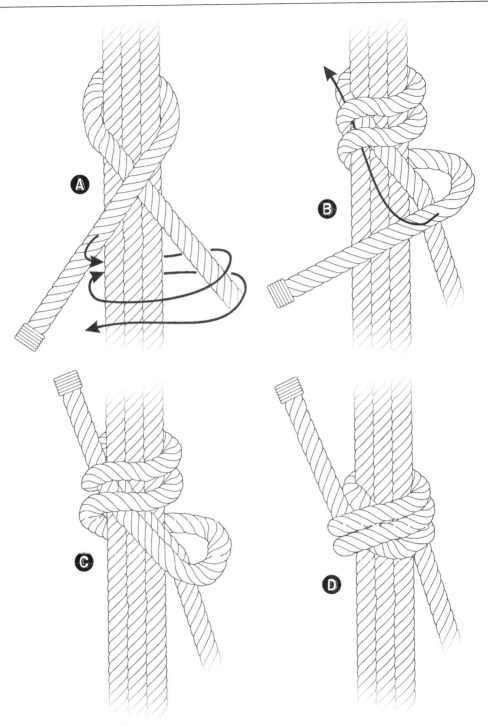

Figure 72. Strangle Knot.

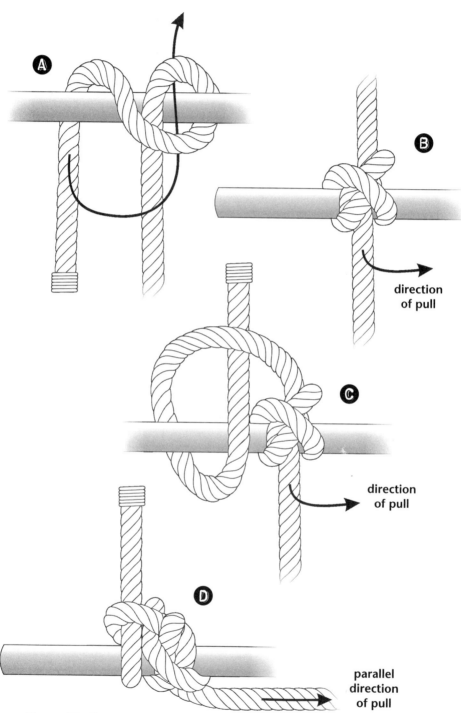

Figure 73. Constrictor Knot.

Hitches

permanent knot. In actual practice, this knot frequently has its ends heat-melted so that it cannot be untied.

To apply the knot, take a turn around the objects to be tied, pass the bitter end over the working part, and take another turn around the objects to the left of the working part as shown in Figure 73A. As the arrow in Figure 73A shows, bring the bitter end over the working part and up under the bottom and top parts of the first turn. Pull tightly on the bitter end and the working part to cinch the knot, as in Figure 73B.

To provide for a parallel pull on the working part, add a half hitch with the bitter end as shown in Figures 73C and 73D. To improve pulling ability still more, add as many consecutive half hitches as required to prevent slipping.

7

Splices

The term *splices* is a little like the term *knots*: it has a general meaning as well as a specific meaning. The general category of splices refers to ropework that is relatively permanent in nature, unlike knots (knots, bends, and hitches), which are usually designed to be tied and untied. Most splices will never be undone. Splices in laid line involve unlaying strands of the line and forming the splice by weaving the strands into the strands of another line or another part of the same line, and splices in braided line involve inserting the bitter end of the line inside another braided line or another part of the same line.

There are three types of spliced ropework: rope ends such as the Back Splice, connecting ropes (splices—the specific meaning) such as the Short Splice, and spliced eyes such as the Eye Splice.

Rope Ends

Spliced rope ends, unlike knots for rope ends, are permanent rope ends, which involve unlaying the rope strands and interweaving them back into the working part of the rope.

Splices

Back Splice

The Back Splice is the most seamanlike method of ending a line to prevent unlaying. Easier methods include a simple heat-melt (pages 17–19), the Strangle Knot (pages 98–99), the Wall and Crown Knot (see below), or the Matthew Walker Knot (pages 110–12). Most sailors prefer the Back Splice's symmetry and firmness.

To make a Back Splice, razor-cut the end of three-strand laid nylon line. Then, apply masking tape to each strand to form points, unlaying approximately 12 to 14 inches of line.

With the unlaid strands, cast a Crown Knot and tighten by pulling and twisting with the lay as in Figures 75C and 75D.

Make a total of five sets of the following tucks:

1. Pick any of the three end strands and go under the adjacent working part strand (Figure 74A).

2. Watch for two parallel strands on the working part (railroad tracks); go over the first and under the second of these strands (Figure 74B).

3. Turn the entire working part, and go over the first and under the second of the working part strands with the third end strand as seen in Figure 74C.

Pull each strand tight with attention to a tight lay. Continue this pattern and shape the splice with your fingers as you go (Figures 74D to 74H).

For decoration, you may end the Back Splice with a Wall and Crown Knot (see below), pulling it tight with pliers (Figure 74I) and hiding the ends by a heat-melt *(dimpling)* as seen in Figure 74J.

Wall and Crown Knot

The Wall and Crown Knot is actually two knots. A Crown Knot is superimposed upon a Wall Knot as a decorative finish to the end of a line.

Figures 75A to 75E are shown looking directly at the end of a three-strand rope. Consider the rest of the rope to be going away directly into the paper.

Knots, Bends, and Hitches for Mariners

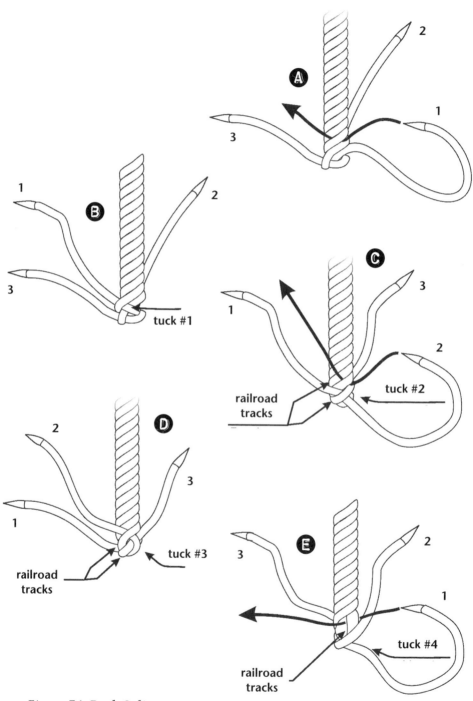

Figure 74. Back Splice.

Splices

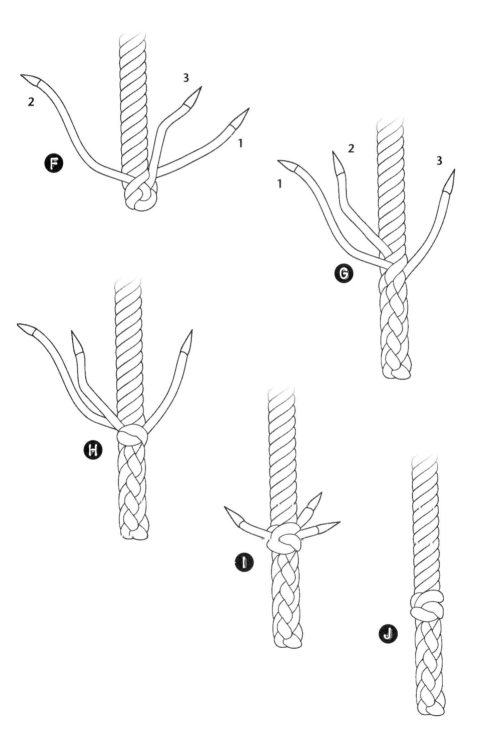

To cast the Wall Knot, begin as in Figure 75A, which shows a three-strand rope end-on, with its strands unlaid for several inches. Then pull and tighten as in Figure 75B. The Crown Knot follows. Cast it as shown in Figure 75C, then pull and tighten as in Figure 75D.

Note that the Crown's weave is exactly opposite the Wall's weave. For example, in the Wall, strand 1 is pulled over and then under strand 3, then up through the loop of strand 2 (Figure 75A).

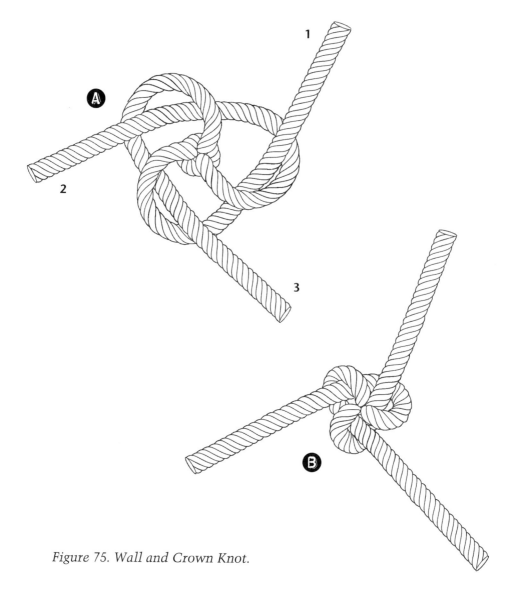

Figure 75. Wall and Crown Knot.

Splices

In the Crown that follows, conversely, strand 1 is pulled under and then over strand 3, then down through the loop of strand 2 as shown in Figure 75C.

After completing the step shown in Figure 75D, heat-cut the free ends of the strands close to the knot and dimple the ends if necessary (Figure 75E).

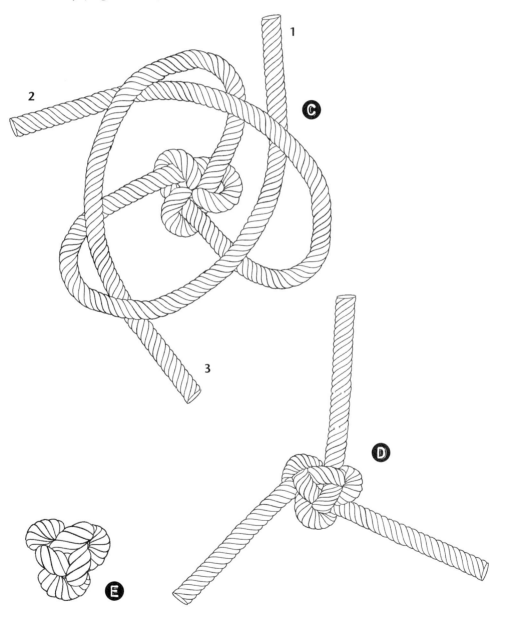

109

Knots, Bends, and Hitches for Mariners

Matthew Walker Knot

This ancient knot is the only one named after a sailor. Following is how Clifford Ashley, in *The Ashley Book of Knots*, describes its origin:

> [Darcy] Lever's familiar expression, 'Matthew Walker's Knot,' suggests that he may have known the inventor, who was possibly a master rigger in one of the British naval dockyards. Many myths have grown up around Matthew Walker, 'the only man ever to have a knot named for him.' Dr. Frederic Lucas, of the American Museum of Natural History, once told me the following story of the origin of the knot, which he had heard off the Chincha Islands while loading guano in 1869.

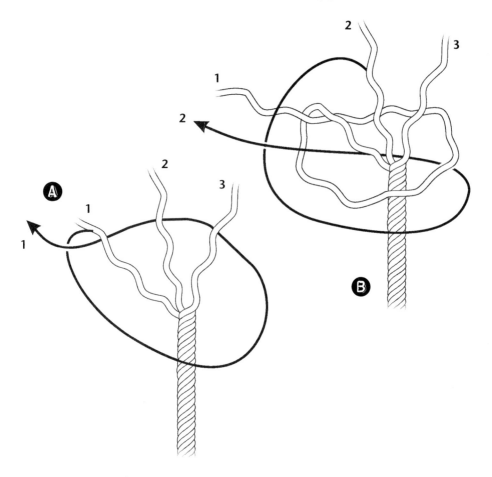

Figure 76. *Matthew Walker Knot.*

Splices

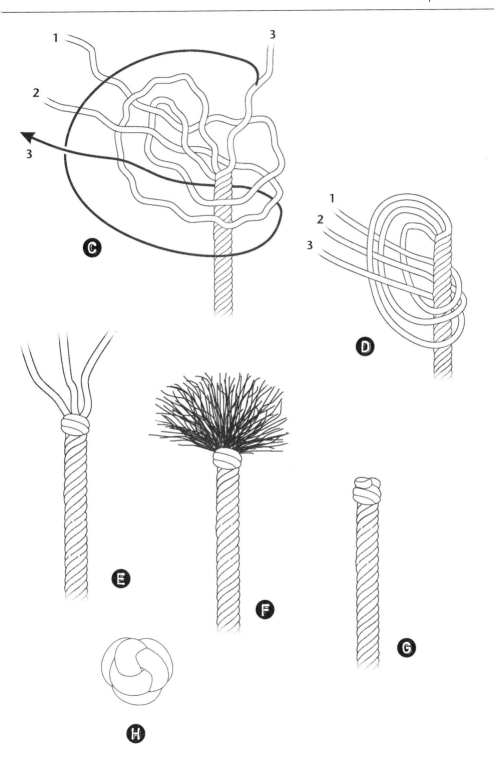

Knots, Bends, and Hitches for Mariners

A sailor, having been sentenced to death by a judge who in earlier life had been a sailor himself, was reprieved by the judge because of their common fellowship of the sea. The judge offered the sailor a full pardon if he could show him a knot that he, the judge, could neither tie nor untie.

The sailor called for ten fathoms of rope and, having retired to the privacy of his cell, unlaid the rope halfway, put in a Matthew Walker Knot, and then laid up the rope again to the end.

So Matthew Walker secured his pardon, and the world gained an excellent knot.

The Matthew Walker Knot is relatively easy to tie but difficult to finish. It is used as a line end to prevent unlaying; as a stopper knot; and/or as part of a bell rope, rope handle, or lanyard. It has also been used for line identification. A great amount of practice is required to cast this knot correctly. Personal instruction is often needed along with patience.

To begin casting the Matthew Walker Knot in ⅜-inch, three-strand laid nylon line, unlay approximately 6 inches, leaving the center strand on top (Figure 76A). Wrap each of the three strand ends with masking tape or heat-melt them to form sealed points.

Place the strands in the positions shown in Figures 76B and 76C. Then, lightly pull up on the strands as you first twist the line below the knot against the lay and then twist the forming knot with the lay of the rope (Figure 76D). Pull tight gradually to the form shown in Figure 76E.

Finish the line with a teased ending, as shown in Figure 76F, or with a Crown ending, as shown in Figures 76G and 76H. Or be creative and come up with a finish of your own.

Connecting Ropes

Splicing can be used to connect two ropes together in a permanent fashion. This method yields a stronger and generally more attractive connection than any knot. Also, a worn section of an otherwise intact long line can be cut out and the cut ends spliced together to extend the life of the line. There will be some loss of strength in doing this (about 15% for the Short Splice) but the line will certainly still be serviceable.

Short Splice

The art of splicing is a challenge, and its final appearance is the reward. Done correctly, the Short Splice is aesthetically pleasing and structurally correct. The Short Splice is stronger than the Long Splice, but increases the diameter of the line, rendering it useless for passing through blocks.

To splice ⅜-inch laid rope, unlay about 8 inches of each end of the lines to be joined, and heat-melt the ends of each strand. Then, intertwine the strands as shown in Figure 77A.

Next, secure the unlaid ends very tightly with a twine Sack Knot (pages 98, 99) as seen in Figure 77B.

Make the first tuck by passing strand 1 over strand 4 and under strand 5. Rotate the splice a bit, and make the second tuck by passing strand 2 over strand 5 and under strand 6 (Figure 77C). Make the third and last tuck by passing strand 3 over strand 6 and under strand 4 (Figure 77D). This completes one set.

Make two more sets of the three tucks described above (Figure 77D). Make sure that all the strands are pulled and twisted with the lay after each set of tucks to snug down the strands in place. This makes the final splice neat and firm.

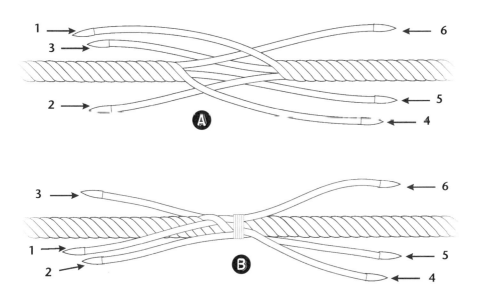

Figure 77. Short Splice.

Knots, Bends, and Hitches for Mariners

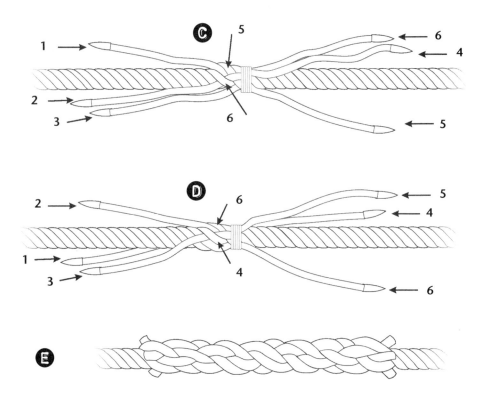

Figure 77 (continued). Short Splice.

Next, turn the splice end-for-end, placing strands 4, 5, and 6 in the positions that strands 1, 2, and 3 were in at the start. Continue making tucks as described until you have made three sets on this side of the Sack Knot (Figure 77E). To avoid any lumpy appearance, remove the twine you wrapped around the unlaid ends (Figure 77B above). Then, place the entire splice on the deck, and roll it back and forth with your foot to smooth it and make it uniform in shape. Heat-cut the protruding ends of the strands and hide them by dimpling.

Long Splice

Knowing how to make a Long Splice is a must for sailors. This splice will pass through a block without jamming because it does not increase the line diameter as a Short Splice does. Repairing a broken halyard with a Long Splice allows the halyard to work as

Splices

easily as before it parted, although it will be a weaker line. This means that the repaired line should be used only as a temporary measure until a replacement can be installed.

To make the Long Splice, first unlay the strands of a ⅜-inch laid line at least 12 inches. Do this carefully to avoid fraying the ends any more than necessary. If desired, use masking tape or twine to temporarily whip the ends of each strand. Next, intertwine the strands as shown in Figure 78A.

Then, loosely tie an Overhand Knot with strands 2 and 5. Make sure that the Overhand Knot follows the configuration shown in Figure 78B. Carefully unlay strand 6 for about 8 inches.

Next, lay strand 3 in the slot created by unlaying strand 6. When strand 3 meets 6, tie them into an Overhand Knot as strands 2 and 5 were tied, but tie this Overhand Knot tightly.

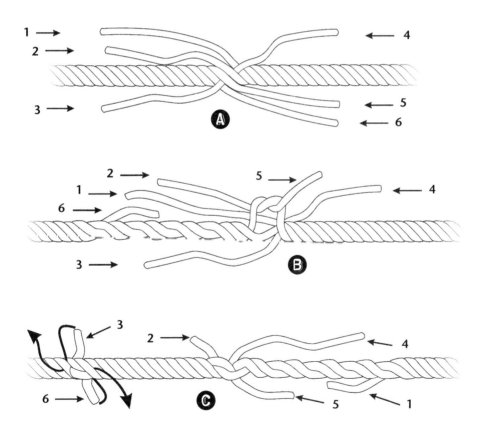

Figure 78. Long Splice.

Knots, Bends, and Hitches for Mariners

Now tighten the Overhand Knot you tied with strands 2 and 5. Examine each strand and its lay to ensure that your work so far is even and equally tight. When this splice is put under tension, each strand must stay in place and take its portion of the load. If they are not equally tight, adjust the tension in the Overhand Knots to correct the loading.

When you have finished these steps, grasp strand 1 and carefully unlay it for about 8 inches.

Lay strand 4 in the slot created by unlaying strand 1. When strand 4 reaches strand 1, tie an Overhand Knot in these two strands as strands 4 and 6 were tied. Again, make this Overhand Knot tight and check the strands for even stress under load (Figure 78C).

Finally, roll the Long Splice on the deck to smooth it and make it appear uniform in shape. When you are satisfied with the result, heat-cut the strands and dimple the ends. The final Long Splice will pass easily through rigging blocks.

Spliced Eyes

Spliced eyes are the strongest and most attractive way to install a loop in the end of a line. This section also describes a method for splicing a loop in the middle of a line.

Eye Splice (Laid Rope)

Eye Splices form permanent loops in the end of laid rope and are usually made 12 to 14 inches long to fit an ordinary cleat or bitt. But they may be any length, such as to fit around a thimble. Strength and beauty are desirable features. Eye Splices for braided rope are covered next.

Start the Eye Splice with the same method used for the Back Splice (pages 105, 106–7). Razor-cut a suitable length of three-strand laid nylon line. Prepare the strands with masking tape twisted to a point. Unlay the line about 10 to 12 inches, leaving the center strand on top.

Make a total of five sets of tucks, as shown in Figure 79D:

- Make the eye loop the desired length on each leg, and start the center strand under the topmost strand of the working part (Figure 79A).

Splices

- Next, place the left strand under the left working part strand and tighten the lay (Figure 79B).
- Turn the entire loop over to see the remaining working part strand. Then, place the third end beneath it, going from right to left (Figure 79C).

For decoration, you may finish the Eye Splice with a Wall and Crown Knot (Figure 79E).

For increased strength, you may add whipping around the throat of the splice. Pulling each strand tight after placing it in its proper position will result in a firm, symmetrical, and handsome Eye Splice. Many variations of the size of the eye and subsequent configurations or uses are possible.

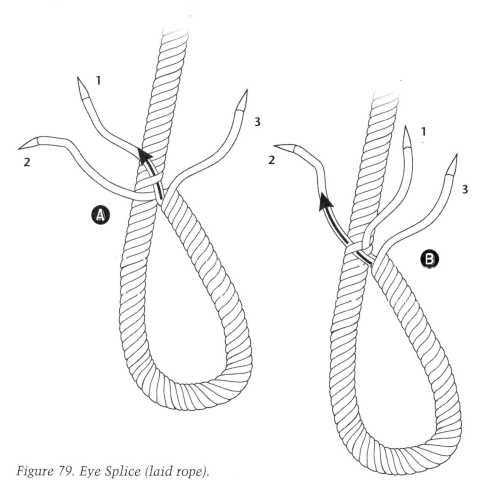

Figure 79. Eye Splice (laid rope).

Knots, Bends, and Hitches for Mariners

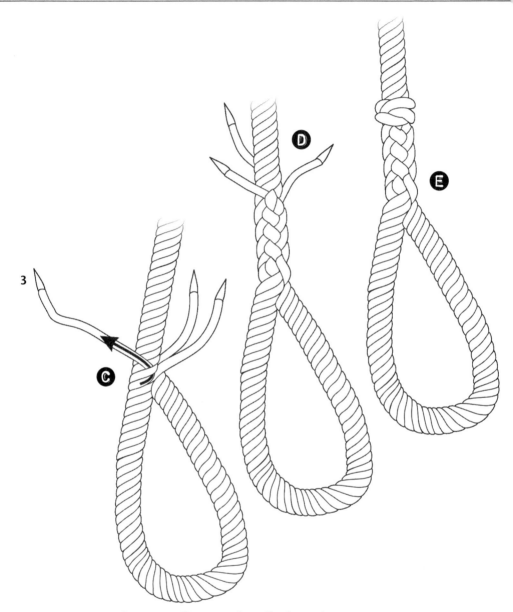

Figure 79 (continued). Eye Splice (laid rope).

Eye Splice (Double-Braid Rope)

Instructions for this Eye Splice call for a hollow or tubular fid. There are other types of fids available, but the hollow fid is one of the most common. It is made in various sizes so you can match the fid to the diameter of rope you're splicing. Since the fid will be used

Splices

to insert either the cover or the core but never both together, use a smaller fid than the rope size; i.e., a ⅜-inch fid for ½-inch rope.

A hollow fid has a pointed end to guide the rope as it is being worked and a slanted hollow end into which the rope is tightly fitted or taped. The fid is divided into short and long sections by marks on its circumference, as shown in Figure 80A.

To begin the Eye Splice, tape the end of the rope and trim it to remove fraying or whipping. Make a mark one full fid length from the end of the line. Label this point R for reference.

Form a loop of the required size and mark the working part opposite point R with an X. At five or more full fid lengths along the working part from point X, tie a tight Slip Knot (pages 37–38, 39) in the line (Figure 80B). This is very important, because it will prevent the core from slipping into the cover as you form the splice.

Returning to point X (Figure 80C), open the strands of the outer cover very carefully, exposing the inner core. Using a nail, ice pick, or similar tool, pull a small section of the core through the cover opening as carefully as possible, marking the core section with a single circumferential mark (mark 1; Figure 80C). Pull out the core carefully until it is completely exposed (Figure 80D). Wrap the core bitter end with tape to prevent unraveling. Now, bunching up the cover, pull out more core from the working part and measure one short fid length from mark 1 on the core. Mark this spot with two circumferential marks (mark 2; Figure 80E).

Continue pulling out the core until you can measure one full fid length plus one short fid length from mark 2. To do this, bunch the cover quite tightly (it may help to insert a nail through the cover and core to keep the cover from slipping back over the core section). Label the core with three circumferential marks at this point (mark 3; Figure 80E). Then, insert the end of the outer cover into the hollow end of the fid, taping it in place if necessary, and insert the fid into the hollow core at mark 2, exiting at mark 3. Continue pulling the cover until point R meets mark 3 (Figure 80E).

Beginning at point R on the cover and moving toward the fid, place a small dot at the fourth intersection of the clockwise and counterclockwise strands that form the cover, a large dot at the eighth intersection (point T), and a small dot at every fourth intersection thereafter (Figure 80E). Cut a single strand at each of the dot locations, beginning at point T. This will serve to taper the cover as the splice continues (Figure 80E).

119

Knots, Bends, and Hitches for Mariners

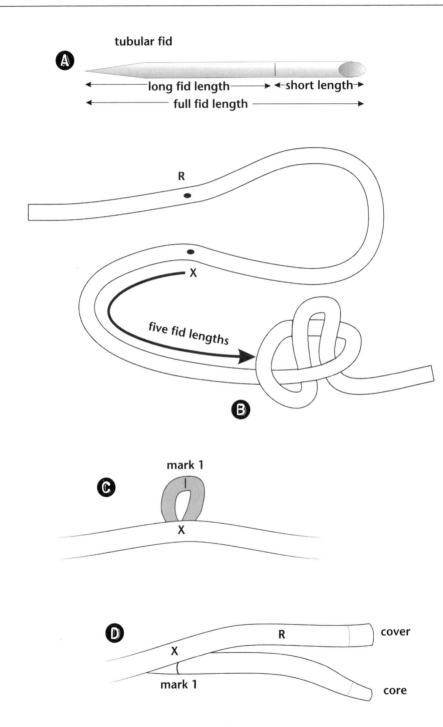

Figure 80. Eye Splice (double-braid rope).

Splices

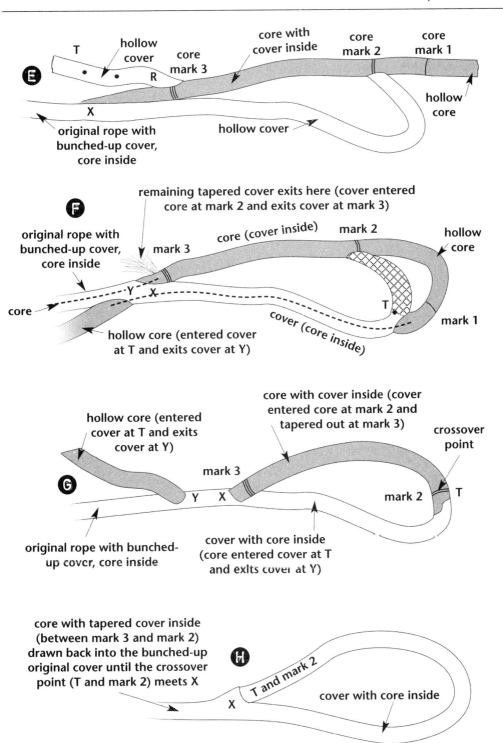

121

Knots, Bends, and Hitches for Mariners

Holding the core, pull the cover back out of the core until the large dot (point T at the beginning of the taper) is exposed (Figure 80F). Be careful not to lose the cover's tapered end in the core. Remove the fid.

Now, insert the end of the core into the fid (use tape, if necessary) and insert the fid into the hollow cover at point T, exiting at point Y, a short fid length from point X toward the Slip Knot (Figure 80F).

Continue to draw the core through the cover, and the cover through the core, until point T and mark 2 are joined at the top of the eye. At this crossover point, smooth the area from the crossover to mark 3, covering the tapered end of the cover (Figure 80G).

Remove the fid, open the cover strands at point X, and make a mark on the core at this point. Make a second mark on the core at point Y, then pull the core until the mark you made at point Y is visible. Now unbraid the core and cut it off at a 45° angle between the two marks. Holding the line at the bottom of the eye, smooth the cover to hide the core tail.

Remove the nail holding the bunched-up cover, and smooth the cover over the core (mark 3 to mark 2) to hide the core and crossover point. Point T should meet point X. Rolling and flexing the line will help in working the line and finishing the splice (Figure 80H).

Eye Splice in the Middle of Laid Line

Before beginning this Eye Splice, decide where in a line you wish to put it. Wrap the spot(s) with masking tape and apply another wrapping of masking tape 20 inches farther along the rope. Twist out the three strands of rope between the marks. These individual strands form a two-strand loop about 10 inches in length. Bring the two tape-marked portions of the rope closely together with the three doubled and twisted-out strands emerging perpendicularly from the point between the marks. Form three sharp points on these ends (Figure 81A). Make an 8-inch loop in the longer portion of the rope.

Begin the splice using the technique described in the Eye Splice in laid line and as shown in Figures 81B, 81C, and 81D. Make the tucks along the longer length of the rope, using the two-stranded material to make the splice rather than the single-

122

Splices

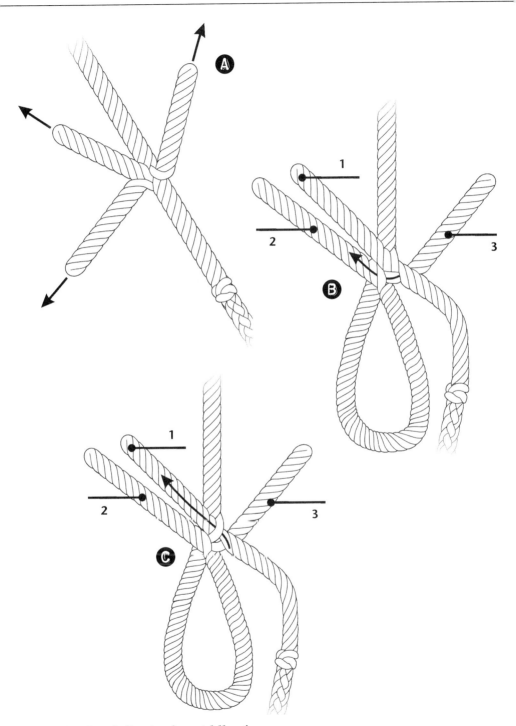

Figure 81. Eye Splice in the middle of rope.

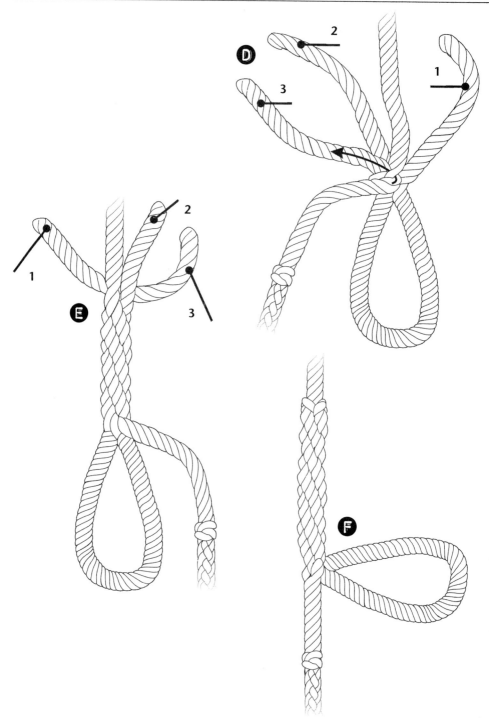

Figure 81 (continued). Eye Splice in the middle of rope.

Splices

strand material described in the Eye Splice in laid line. Continue the splice for four or five tucks with the double-stranded material (Figure 81E). End this splice by thoroughly heat-melting the ends in place (Figure 81F). You can add as many spliced eyes as are needed.

8

Decorative Knots

Decorative knots are more than simply beautiful; they also serve useful purposes, as described in this chapter.

Line Ends

Decorative line ends can be either knots (like the Turk's Head) or splices (like the Tack Knot or Star Knot). Either way, their attractive appearance is the reward for the effort required to cast them.

Turk's Head

This decorative seaman's knot has the appearance of a turban. It has some intrinsic beauty and is used to cover a portion of bell rope or chest handle. It also may be used to mark a position on a line or helm wheel.

To make this knot, you must have the continuous line in the proper position as indicated in the illustrations. Then, pull the entire knot tight, tuck by tuck.

When studying the illustrations, keep in mind that when you are looking at the back of the hand, you can see fingernails and the thumb is down. When you see the thumb up and no nails, you

Decorative Knots

are looking at the palm of the hand. This shows you when to turn your hand over when making the knot.

Start the knot as shown, holding it in place as necessary with your thumb (Figure 82A).

Turn your hand over. Place the bitter end under strand 1 and over strand 2 (Figure 82B).

Transpose strand 1 under 2, and hold in position with your fourth finger (Figure 82C).

Now, pass the bitter end under strand 1 and over strand 2 (Figure 82D).

Turn your hand over. Pass the bitter end under strand 1 and over strand 2 (Figure 82E).

Continue with the bitter end going under strand 1, and finish the knot following the trace of the basic pattern laid out in the previous steps (Figure 82F).

Three complete rounds are required to complete the knot (Figure 82G).

Tuck by tuck, draw up the strands firmly—but not too tightly—against a short wooden dowel as a form. At this point, heat-melt the two ends and hide them in the knot. After removing the Turk's Head from the dowel form, permanently secure the ends with a drop of white glue applied to each end from the inside.

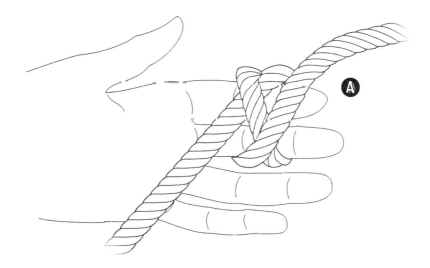

Figure 82. Turk's Head.

Knots, Bends, and Hitches for Mariners

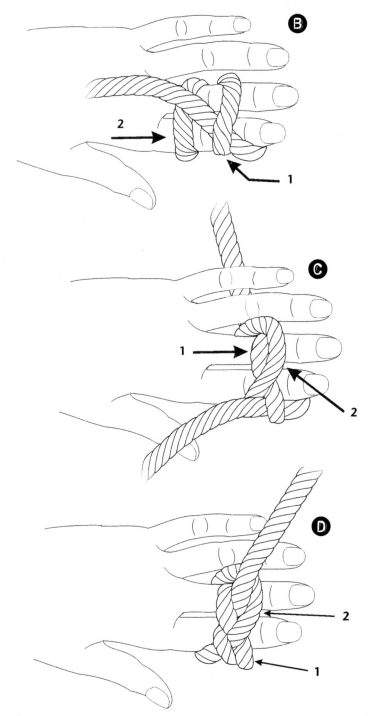

Figure 82 (continued). Turk's Head.

Decorative Knots

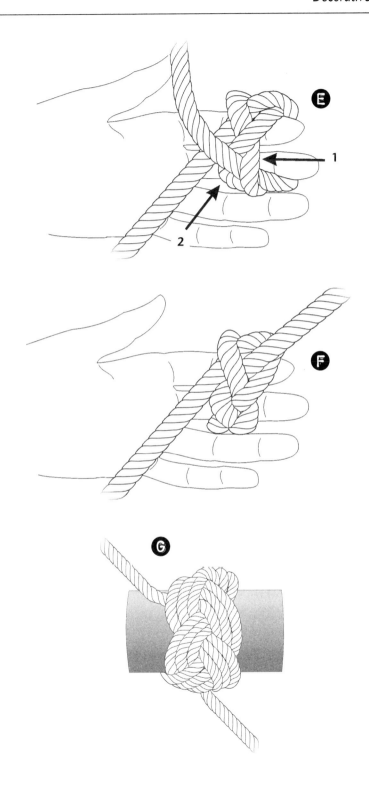

Knots, Bends, and Hitches for Mariners

Crown Sennit

What is a sennit? *Webster's Unabridged Dictionary* provides this definition:

> **sen•nit** (sen´nit), *n.* [*seven* + *knit*] A flat, braided cordage, formed by plaiting strands of line, yarn, or other fiber, used as small stuff.

We'll define the Crown Sennit as a decorative continuous series of Crown Knots that can be used alone or to cover another line or object. Results will vary since you can change the number of strands and colors as well as the direction of the strands and endings.

CASTING THE CROWN SENNIT

This Crown Sennit is a five-stranded, right-turned (counterclockwise, as viewed from above) Crown Sennit covering a laid nylon line. Select the strands you will use in the Sennit cover. Allow 4 inches of each strand to cover 1 inch of ⅜-inch line. Secure the five strands to the end of the core line with a Twice- or Thrice-Turned Sack Knot (pages 98–100). Heat-cut and heat-melt the end of the core line and the five strands together (Figure 83A). The Crown Sennit effect is accomplished by casting a series of Crown Knots (pages 108–9) working from the bitter end of the core line toward the working part.

Start the first series of five tucks (Crowns to the left) and pull tight (Figures 83B, 83C, and 83D). Repeat this series of five tucks, pulling them tightly, for as many times as you need to cover the desired core length (Figure 83E).

To finish, heat-melt each strand. Any other knot with a central core, such as a Tack Knot (see below) or Star Knot (pages 132, 135–39), can be heat-melted to either end of this Sennit, as long as there will be no load on it.

Tack Knot

The Tack Knot is sometimes used as a decorative method of forming a stopper or knob in a line or at its end. It may be made from the core line end or using strands from another line joined to the core line by whipping. The Tack Knot is then heat-melted to the line to be decorated.

Basically, it is a Wall and Crown Knot (pages 105, 108–9),

Decorative Knots

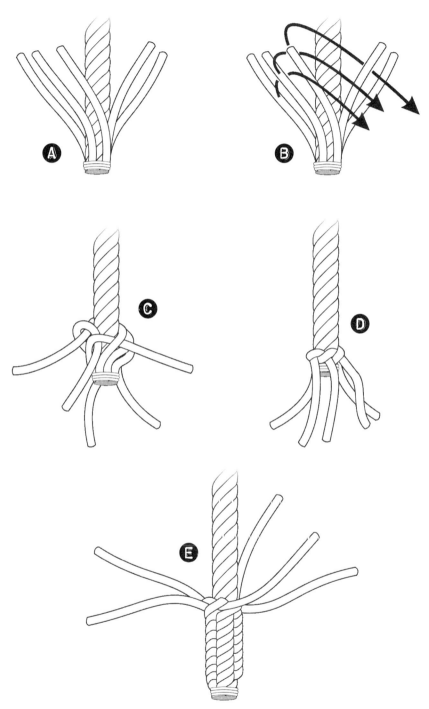

Figure 83. Crown Sennit.

Knots, Bends, and Hitches for Mariners

doubled. It has many uses, limited only by your imagination. It is suitable for bell ropes, chest handles, line identification, a bucket rope, or decorative rope jewelry.

To tie this knot, you may use three to six strands—five strands are shown in the illustrations. Prepare the strands, each about 8 inches long, and whip them together with a Thrice-Turned Sack Knot (Figure 84A). Heat-seal appropriately.

With the top up, cast a five-tuck Wall Knot by working the strands in a counterclockwise direction (Figure 84B). Be sure that all of the strands follow this same counterclockwise direction throughout all the steps. After the strands are positioned loosely, tighten them slowly and firmly (Figure 84C).

With the top up, make a Crown by passing each strand (in a counterclockwise direction) over the adjacent strand to the left. Tighten slowly but firmly (Figure 84D).

Keep the top of the knot up (still working in a counterclockwise direction). Pull each strand behind the adjacent strand, then up through the adjacent loop using a hemostat (Figures 84E and 84F).

After the strands have all been pulled loosely through the loops, slowly tighten each strand, again working in a counterclockwise direction, until it is snug, as shown in Figures 84G and 84H.

With the top of the knot still up, find your way down through the knot with a fid. Moving counterclockwise and using a hemostat, pull the strands through and out of the bottom. After you have pulled all of the strands through, tighten them (Figures 84I and 84J).

Pull each strand tightly with pliers, working in a counterclockwise direction. Heat-cut the excess ends and melt the ends into the knot. Finally, shape the knot by pressing its edges against a table (Figure 84K).

Finish the knot professionally by filling the center hole with a two-strand plug. Use a small drop of white glue to hold it in place (Figure 84L).

Practice this knot to perfect the technique before trying the even more intricate Star Knot that follows.

Star Knot

The Star Knot is perhaps the favorite decorative knot of all marlinespike seamanship enthusiasts. Many knot historians agree that this knot has been recorded and admired for centuries.

132

Decorative Knots

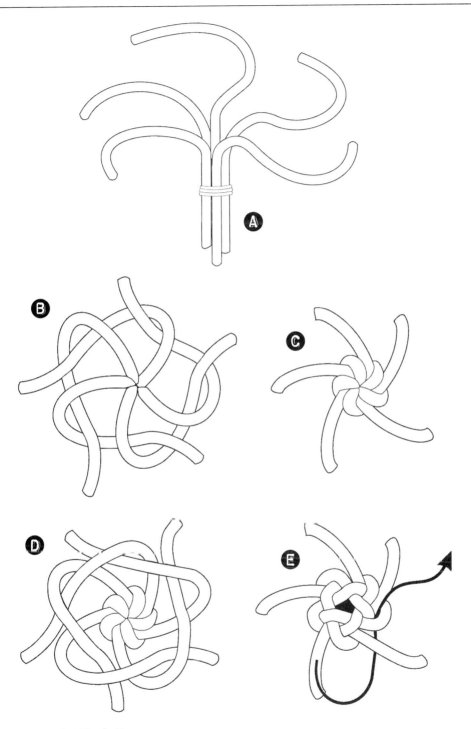

Figure 84. Tack Knot.

Knots, Bends, and Hitches for Mariners

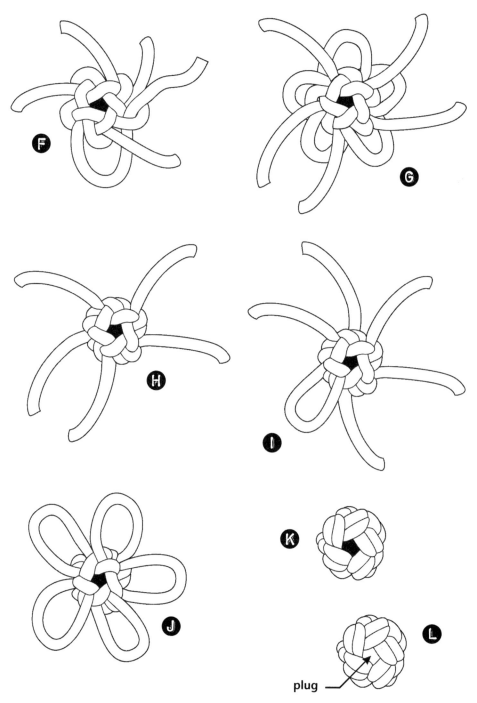

Figure 84 (continued). Tack Knot.

Decorative Knots

Due to its intricate nature, the Star Knot is not encountered every day, nor is it commonly in the repertoire of the average sailor. Because of its complexity, it will require many attempts to master, but when you cast this knot, you will be highly respected within the marlinespike seamanship ranks. The knot is primarily decorative, but a little imagination will reveal many uses. For example, it is excellent as the end of a Bell Rope Sennit (pages 140–42).

The first two steps of this knot are done in a clockwise direction, exactly the opposite to the method used to cast a Tack Knot. Also, except as noted, all of the following illustrations are viewed from the top of the knot.

A Five-Strand Star Knot is described here.

The first step is to join the five strands by whipping them together as shown in Figure 85A.

With the top up, start by making an underhand loop in one of the strands (Figure 85B). Then, proceed clockwise and make an underhand loop in the next strand. Pass the end of the strand up through the previous loop from the back (Figure 85C). Continue doing the same for each strand, working in a clockwise direction. After all the strands have been looped, tighten slowly and firmly (Figure 85D).

With the top still up, pass each strand clockwise over the next strand. Working clockwise, continue this process for all the strands, then tighten each strand while working the knot. Ensure that all strands are tight (Figure 85E).

With the top still up, and now working counterclockwise, thread the first strand as shown in Figures 85F and 85G. Use a fid to thread the strand and a mosquito hemostat to pull it through. Do not tighten the strands until you can tighten all strands together slowly. Shape the knot as you tighten (Figure 85H).

Turn the knot over, bottom up, to proceed. Using a fid and mosquito hemostat, thread each strand down through the hole shown in Figure 85I. Do not tighten any of the strands until all the strands have been pulled down and through. Proceed in a clockwise direction, and shape the knot as you tighten the strands (Figure 85J).

Turn the knot over again so the top is up (Figure 85K). Use a fid and hemostat to thread each strand down and through the hole as shown in Figure 85K. After all strands have been fed through,

Knots, Bends, and Hitches for Mariners

tighten each strand, working slowly clockwise until they are tight and the knot is firm (Figure 85L).

Turn the knot over again so the bottom is up. With a fid and mosquito hemostat, thread each strand through or under the two strands shown in Figures 85M to 85P. Do not tighten the strands at this stage.

After all the strands have been fed through, and with the bottom still up, tighten each strand slowly and firmly (Figure 85Q). Be sure to work in a clockwise direction. Note that after tightening the strands are ready to be trimmed and hidden (Figure 85R).

With the bottom up, heat-cut each strand carefully, then heat-melt the strand ends inside the knot (Figure 85S).

To ensure that the final product is nautically attractive and correct, make certain that you continually shape the knot as you cast it (Figure 85T).

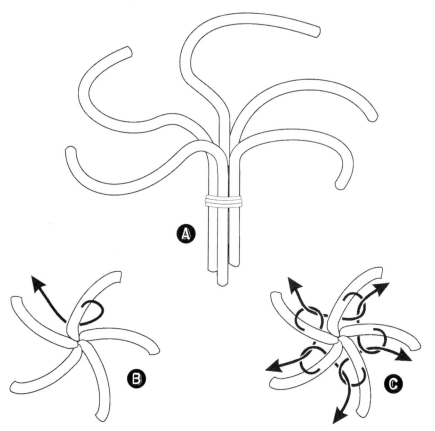

Figure 85. Star Knot.

Decorative Knots

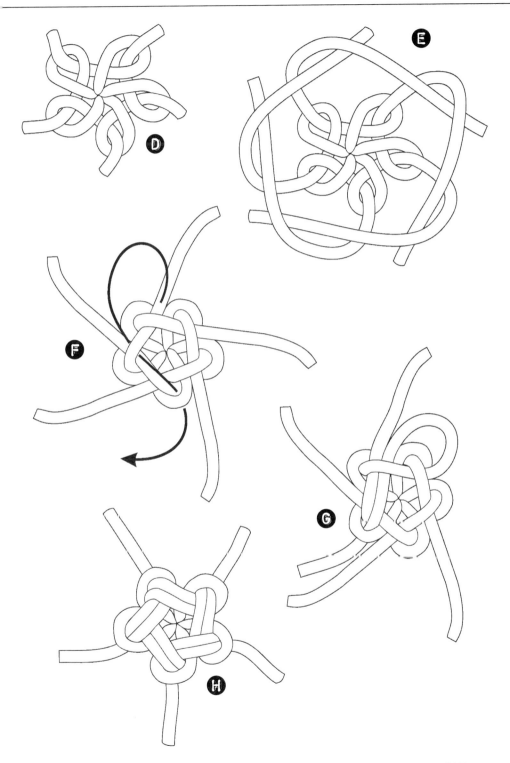

Knots, Bends, and Hitches for Mariners

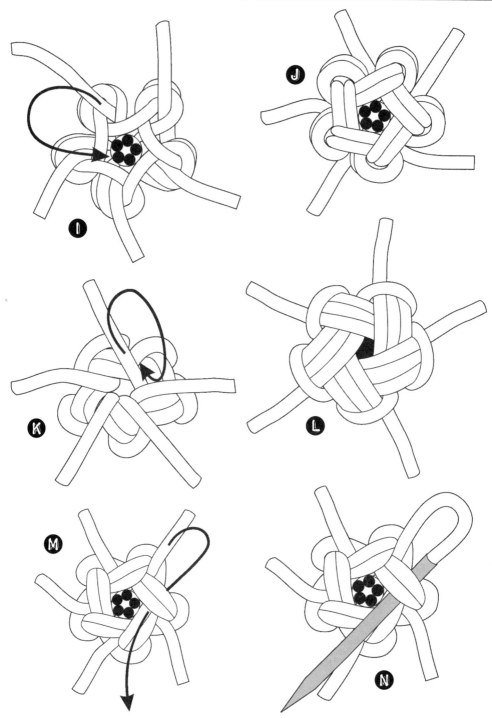

Figure 85 (continued). Star Knot.

Decorative Knots

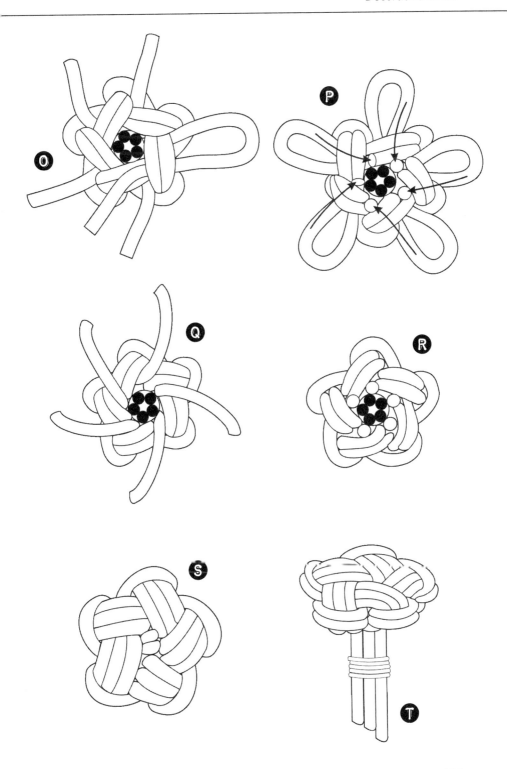

Knots, Bends, and Hitches for Mariners

Bell Rope Sennit

This Sennit is designed to test your ability to cast four different knots that have been described in this text. They are the Matthew Walker Knot (pages 110–12), Crown Sennit (pages 130, 131; here you'll cast a Six-Strand Crown Sennit), Tack Knot (pages 130, 132, 133–34), and the Star Knot (pages 132, 135–39).

For this knot, you will use many of the line management techniques that you have learned thus far, and you will also be dyeing several of the lines. But don't worry; just follow the instructions below and you'll be able to accomplish each stage of the process.

Nylon ropes and twine required:
¼-inch braided
³⁄₁₆-inch braided
⅛-inch braided
⅜-inch twisted laid rope
¹⁄₁₆-inch twine (small stuff)—used to secure the strands of
 Tack Knots or Star Knots and for starting the Six-
 Strand Crown Sennit

Cut the line in the following approximate lengths:

For the Six-Strand Crown Sennit:
One 14-inch piece of ⅜-inch twisted nylon rope—for the center of the Six-Strand Crown Sennit
One 36-inch piece of ¹⁄₁₆-inch braided rope—for the tapered padding at the center of the Six-Strand Crown Sennit
Six pieces, each 36 inches long, of ⅛-inch rope—for the dyed cover of the Six-Strand Crown Sennit—dyed as two dark colors, two medium colors, and two light colors

For the Tack Knot:
Five pieces, each 14 inches long, of ³⁄₁₆-inch rope
Two short 3-inch strands of ¹⁄₁₆-inch twine (small stuff), for holding a stainless steel oval ring

For the Star Knot:
Six strands of ¼-inch braided nylon rope, each 15 inches long—dyed as two dark, two medium, and two light colors

140

Decorative Knots

CREATING THE BELL ROPE SENNIT

Tie a Matthew Walker Knot in each end of the ⅜-inch twisted laid rope so that the final result of this segment is 4 inches long (Figure 86A).

Wind a piece of the 1/16-inch braided twine (small stuff) up 2½ inches from the bottom Matthew Walker Knot, or about forty wraps (Figure 86B). Then, wind another piece of the 1/16-inch braided twine over the first wrapping up from the bottom 1¼ inches, or about twenty wraps.

Heat-melt the six strands of dyed ⅛-inch line at the base of the core, as shown in Figure 86C.

Make a Six-Strand Crown Sennit from these strands up to the top Matthew Walker Knot (Figure 86D).

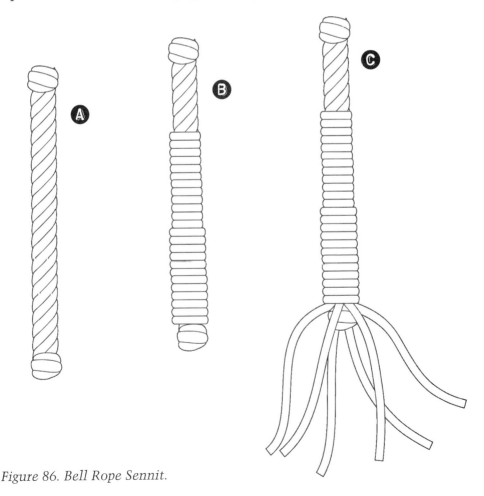

Figure 86. Bell Rope Sennit.

141

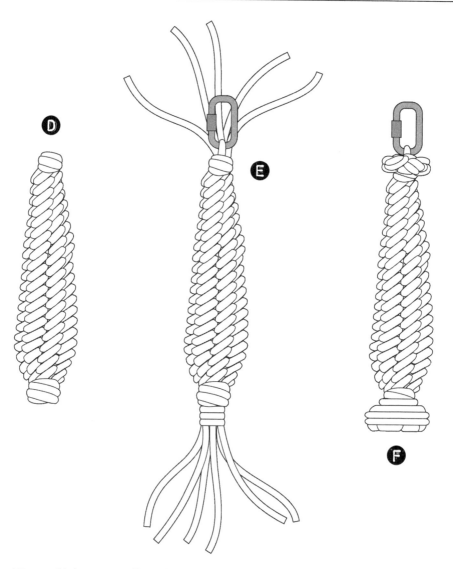

Figure 86 (continued). Bell Rope Sennit.

Prepare a five-strand Tack Knot by first heat-melting the strands and ring to the top Matthew Walker Knot, then casting the knot (Figure 86E).

Prepare a six-strand Star Knot by first heat-melting the strands to the bottom Matthew Walker Knot, then casting the knot.

Use a padded vise to shape the entire Bell Rope Sennit (Figure 86F).

Decorative Knots

Cockscombing

This ancient ropework was originally used as chafing gear and as covers for deck rigs and handrails. Now we use it as a rope cover for decorative purposes, such as framing. The work can be beautifully accentuated if you are precise, pull each tuck tight, position the front braiding, and make no mistakes. Cut the length of line to be covered. Then select the type, colors, and desired length of the Cockscombing line. Secure the lines with a Twice- or Thrice-Turned Sack Knot (pages 98–100) and heat-melt the ends (Figure 87A).

Place the line to be covered in a vertical position and pull the line cover strands down. Make the first set of tucks as follows:

- Left strand: Go right, in front, and around back, ending under the same strand (right half hitch; Figure 87B).
- Middle strand: Go left, in front, and around back, ending under the same strand (left half hitch; Figure 87C).
- Right strand: Go right and around back, ending under the same strand (right half hitch; Figure 87D).

Be careful to pull each strand tight after the half hitch. From that point on, use the formula:

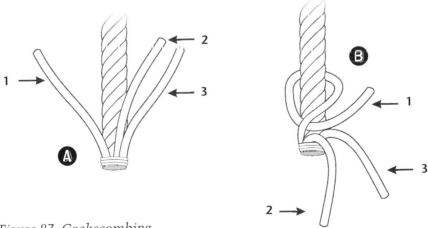

Figure 87. Cockscombing.

143

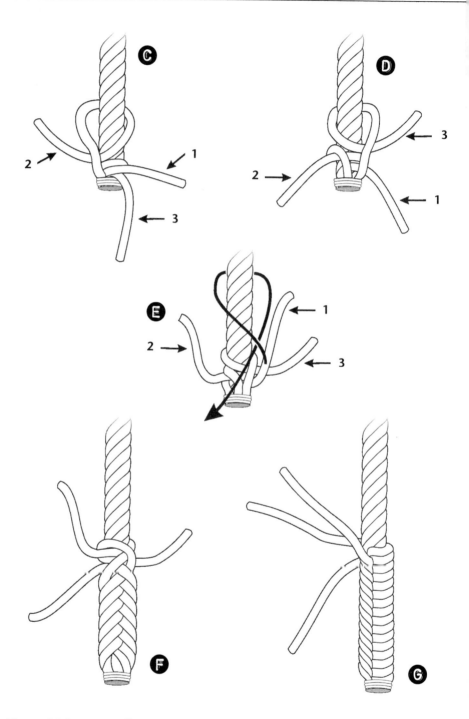

Figure 87 (continued). Cockscombing.

Decorative Knots

- Lowest strand on the right side: Go up front, around back, and under the same strand (left half hitch; Figure 87E).

- Lowest strand on the left side: Go up front, around back, and under the same strand (right half hitch; Figures 87F and 87G).

To finish, heat-melt all the ends or cover them with whipping.

Toggle Knots

When you need a temporary, quick, and convenient knot that can bear a continuous load and also be rapidly untied, even under load, think of a Toggle Knot (see, for example, Figure 88C). You will need to prepare the toggles ahead of time to use them most efficiently (see Figures 31, 32A, and 32B on pages 35–36). Many knots can be toggled, and three intriguing possibilities are described on the following pages. Incidentally, when you make a toggle, make certain it is strong enough to stand the strain you intend to apply to the Toggle Knot. If you fail in this regard, catastrophe can strike in an instant.

Toggled Reef Knot

To produce a Toggled Reef Knot, any fixed loops will do, but the ends of the loops must be secure. It is ideal for joining two Eye Splices, the loops of any loop-producing knots, or any combination of loops.

Cast the Toggled Reef Knot by taking the tip of one loop through the tip of a second loop, bringing them together from opposite directions (Figure 88A). Press the legs of the second loop up through the first loop and hold them in position.

Place the toggle between the legs of the second loop in front and the legs of the first loop behind (Figure 88B).

Draw up tightly and maintain constant pressure on the toggle (Figure 88C).

Toggled Lark's Head

The same uses apply to the Toggled Lark's Head as to its untoggled counterpart, the Lark's Head (pages 92–93). Procure a ring large enough to fit over the doubled line used for the knot.

145

Knots, Bends, and Hitches for Mariners

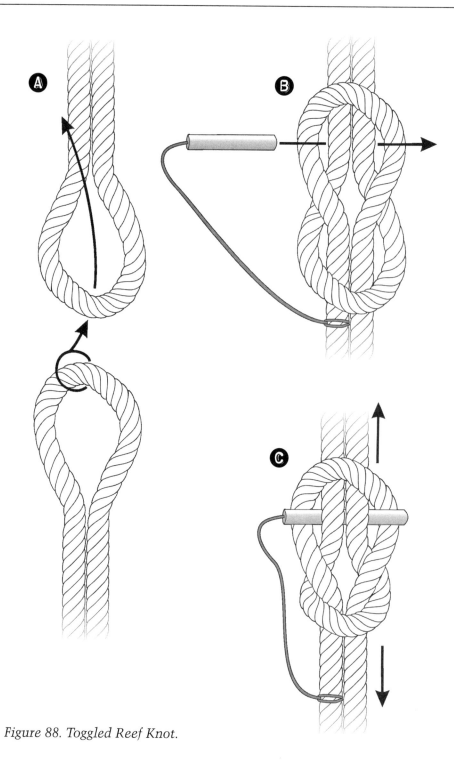

Figure 88. Toggled Reef Knot.

Decorative Knots

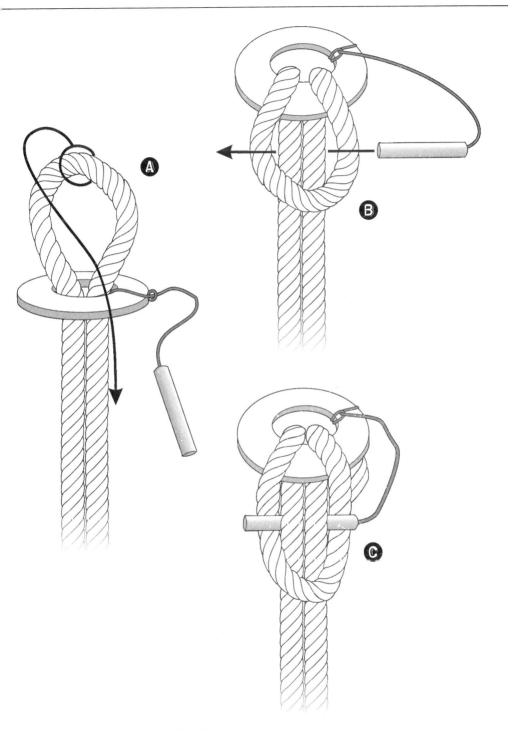

Figure 89. Toggled Lark's Head.

With the ring and toggle ready, form a bight with its legs together as seen in Figure 89A. Pull the bight through the ring and down over the legs. Push the legs forward through the bight and hold them there. Position the toggle behind the legs where you pulled them through the bight, but in front of the bight (Figure 89B). Pull down on the legs to tighten the bight and the legs against the toggle (Figure 89C). Even pressure must be applied to the load on the legs to maintain the integrity of the knot.

Toggle and Becket

There may be occasions when you wish to secure or hang a long, heavy coiled line in one location by buttoning the toggle in the loop. For example, you can coil the line and secure it with a Toggle and Becket that is wrapped around a spar.

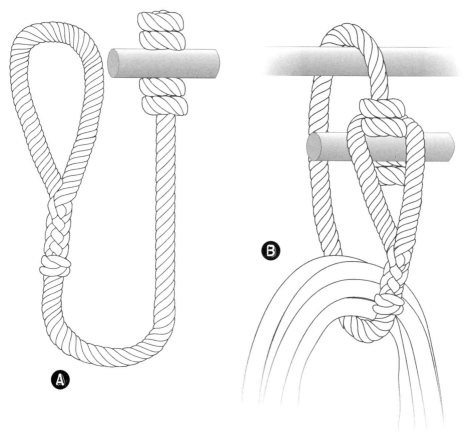

Figure 90. Toggle and Becket.

Decorative Knots

Prepare a toggle using a ¾-inch-diameter hardwood dowel. Drill a ⅜-inch hole through the dowel perpendicular to its center. Thread ⅜-inch line through the hole. Cast a Blood Knot (pages 41–42) in the end of the line and heat-seal it.

Cast a second Blood Knot in the same line and draw the second knot tightly against the opposite side of the dowel, leaving the line stopped against opposite sides of the dowel. Allow a sufficient length of line to go around the coil and make an Eye Splice in the opposite end of the line. Finish that splice with a dimpled Wall and Crown Knot (Figure 90A).

To use this device, simply bring the Eye Splice loop up and around a spar and the line, hose, electrical cord, etc. being hung. Then, "button" in the toggle. Release the coil by "unbuttoning" the toggle (Figure 90B).

149

Bibliography

Ashley, Clifford W. With amendments by Geoffrey Budworth. *The Ashley Book of Knots*. New York: Doubleday, 1993.

Avery, Derek E. *The New Encyclopedia of Knots*. London: Brockhampton, 2001.

Budworth, Geoffrey. *The Complete Book of Knots*. New York: Lyons and Burford, 1997. Published simultaneously in Great Britain as *The Hamlyn Book of Knots*. London: Hamlyn, 1997.

Cassidy, John. *The Klutz Book of Knots: How to Tie the World's 24 Most Useful Hitches, Ties, Wraps, and Knots*. Palo Alto, California: Klutz Press, 1985.

Cutler, Thomas J. *The Bluejacket's Manual: United States Navy*. Centennial ed. Annapolis, Maryland: Naval Institute Press, 2002.

Day, Cyrus L. *The Art of Knotting and Splicing*. Edited by Ray O. Beard. Jr. and M. Lee Hoffman Jr. 4th ed. Annapolis, Maryland: Naval Institute Press, 1986.

Fry, Eric C. *The Complete Book of Knots and Ropework*. Newton Abbot, England: David and Charles, 2004.

Gibbs, Tony. *Practical Sailing*. New York: Motor Boating and Sailing Books, 1971.

Jarman, Colin. *The Essential Knot Book: Knots, Bends, Hitches, Whippings, Splices*. 3rd ed. Camden, Maine: International Marine, 2004.

Maloney, Elbert S. *Chapman Piloting: Seamanship and Small Boat Handling*. 64th ed. New York: Hearst Books, 2003.

Merry, Barbara. *The Splicing Handbook: Techniques for Modern and Traditional Ropes*. 2nd ed. Camden, Maine: International Marine, 2000.

Smith, Hervey Garrett. *The Marlinspike Sailor*. Camden, Maine: International Marine, 1993.

Wing, Charlie. *Captain's Quick Guide: Knots, Splices, and Line Handling*. Camden, Maine: International Marine, 2004.

Glossary

Anchor: Device used to secure a boat to the bottom of a body of water.

Becket: 1. An *eye* in the end of a *block* for securing a *line*. 2. An eye, usually spliced, in the end of a line.

Belay: 1. To secure a *line* without a *knot* or *hitch*. 2. To make fast by winding a line around a *cleat* or belaying pin.

Bend: A *knot* to secure a *line* to another line.

Bight: *Rope* doubled back on itself to form a *loop* with parallel legs.

Bitt: A strong vertical wood or metal post through the deck, usually with a crossbar, for securing *lines* and cables for mooring or towing.

Bitter end: 1. The inboard end of a *line,* chain, or cable; the end is made fast to the vessel as opposed to the *working part*, which may be attached to an *anchor, cleat,* or other vessel. 2. The rope end hanging out of a *knot* that carries no load.

Block: A rope-pulley assembly, including a frame with an *eye*, for attaching a *line* and one or more rope *sheaves* with axles.

Bollard: A stout post on a deck, wharf, or pier for securing mooring lines.

Capsize: Altering the appearance, shape, or function of a *knot* by changing only the strain.

Cast: To tie a *knot*.

Chafe: Wear on a *line* that is prevented by chafing gear with sacrificial coverings such as leather, cloth, or rubber.

Chock: A fitting to guide a *line* or cable.

Cleat: A fitting, usually with two projecting horns, to which *lines* are made fast.

Cordage: A general term for all types of *rope*.

Dimpling: A method of hiding the rope or strand ends in the last step of *casting* a *knot* or splicing. The rope or strand end is heat-melted to a moldable condition so it can be formed and pressed between the adjacent rope strands with a tool or gloved finger.

Glossary

Eye: A closed permanent *loop* in hardware or in a *line*.

Eyelet: A small *grommet* through which lacing is passed.

Fibers: The smallest division of material in a *rope*. See also *yarns*.

Fid: A tapered tool used in splicing. See also *marlinespike*.

Grommet: A metal ring fitted into a hole in a sail or in canvas.

Hawser: A heavy *rope* or cable used for various purposes such as towing or mooring large vessels.

Hitch: A *knot* used to secure a *line* fast to another object. See also *bend*.

Hockle: A short, tight *bend* or *hitch* in a *rope* or *line* that has been twisted too hard or drawn off a coil too fast.

Knot: 1. A term for securing a *line* to itself. 2. The general term for securing a line to an object, another line, or itself.

Lay: The direction in which a line's *strands* are twisted.

Line: A general term for *rope* used aboard a boat, but especially rope used for a specific function.

Loop: A rope configuration where the legs of a *bight* cross.

Marlinespike: A pointed steel tool used in splicing to open the *strands* or a *rope* or cable. See also *fid*.

Painter: A *line* tied to a bow or a dinghy to tow or secure it.

Pile: A pole or post driven vertically into the bottom usually to support a pier or float or to moor a boat.

Rope: *Cordage* made of natural or synthetic *fibers*; can also be made of steel wire.

Round turn: A complete turn (about 1½ times) of *line* around a *cleat, bitt,* or post.

Seize: To bind together two adjacent *lines* by many small wrappings of small line.

Sennit: A decorative rope configuration, done by hand-braiding the *strands*. Usually flat but may also be round.

Sheave: (pronounced "shiv") The grooved wheel over which a *line* passes as it goes through a *block*.

Slip: A method of using a part of a *line* as a *toggle*, usually by using a *bight* instead of the line end in the last step of *casting* a *knot*.

Small stuff: Light *line* (marline, waxed twine, etc.) used for *whipping, seizing,* and serving.

Stopper: A *knot* at the end of a *line* to keep the line from slipping through a hole or a *block*.

Strand: One of the principal components of a *rope*. See also *yarns*.

Glossary

Thimble: A grooved metal loop around which a *rope* or wire rope may be spliced, thus making the spliced *eye* more *chafe* resistant.

Toggle: A small, wooden crosspiece at the end of a *line* passed through an *eye* or *loop* in another line, as when *bending* a flag onto a halyard.

Unlay: To separate the *strands* of a *rope.*

Whip: To bind the end of a *rope* with light *line* to prevent it from fraying.

Working part: The part of a *rope* that is under load. If used to support a mast on a sailboat it may also be called "standing rigging." If reeved through a *block* it may also be called "running rigging" or "the running part." See also *bitter end.*

Yarns: The intermediate parts comprising laid *rope.* The *fibers* are bundled and twisted in one direction into yarns, which are then bundled and twisted in the opposite direction into *strands,* which are then bundled and twisted in the original direction into rope.

Index

Anchor Bend, 82, 85–86
anchor rodes, 4, 16, 26
Angler's Loop (Perfection Knot), 7, 8, 50, 52–53
aramid fiber rope, 12
The Ashley Book of Knots (Ashley), 110, 112
attaching hitch instructions, 78–97
    Anchor Bend, 82, 85–86
    Bitt Hitch (Tugboat Hitch), 91–92
    Buntline Hitch, 88, 89
    Cleat Hitch, 82, 84
    Clove Hitch for short piles, 82, 83
    Clove Hitch for tall piles, 80–82
    Cow Hitch (Lark's Head), 92–93
    Inside Cow Hitch, 93–95
    Jar Sling, 95–97
    Jug Sling Knot, 95–97
    Lark's Head (Cow Hitch), 92–93
    Rolling Hitch, 86–88
    Round Turn with Two Half Hitches, 78–80
    Slipped Buntline Hitch, 88, 90–91
    Tugboat Hitch (Bitt Hitch), 91–92

Back Splice, 10, 105, 106–7
backward loop, 7
Becket Bend (Becket Hitch), 68, 70, 72
bell rope, 4
Bell Rope Sennit, 19, 135, 140–42
bends, 9, 10
bends, sharp. *See* kinked line
bends, tying instructions for
    Becket Bend (Becket Hitch), 68, 70, 72

Carrick Bend, 72–74
    Double Sheet Bend, 68, 70, 71
    Hawser Bend, 74–76
    Reef (Square) Knot, 76–77
    Sheet Bend, 68–70
    Square (Reef) Knot, 76–77
bight, 4–5
Binder's Loop, 97–98
bitter end, 4
Bitt Hitch (Tugboat Hitch), 91–92
Blood Knot, 37, 41–42, 149
Bowline, 7
    effect of, on line, 9
    half hitch with, 8
    purpose of, 9–10
    tying instructions, 46, 47
Bowline variations
    Bowline on a Bight, 4, 46, 48–50
    Japanese Bowline, 57–59
    Painter's Bowline, 50, 54
    Slipped Bowline, 46, 50, 51
    Spanish Bowline, 55–56
braided rope
    construction, 14–15
    Eye Splice, 118–22
breaking strength of line, 8, 13
Buntline Hitch, 7, 88, 89
    Slipped Buntline Hitch, 88, 90–91

capsizing (knots), 24
Carrick Bend, 72–74
casting a knot, 3
chafe protection, 27–28
chemicals, protecting lines from, 26
clamps, spring, 33
Cleat Hitch, 10, 82, 84

154

Index

Clove Hitch
 Buntline Hitch and, 88
 effect of, on line, 9
 half hitch with, 8, 80, 82
 purpose of, 10
 as Sack Knot, 98
 seizing lines, 24
 for short piles, 82, 83
 for tall piles, 80–82
 uses for, 48
Clover Knot (True Lover's Knot),
  61–63
Cockscombing, 10, 19, 143–45
coiling line, 29–30
cold-cutting rope, 17
connecting line. See also bends,
  tying instructions for
 joining, 19–20
 seizing lines, 24–25
 splices for, 112–16
 Toggled Reef Knot, 145, 146
Constrictor Knot
 half hitch with, 8
 jury-rigging a mast, 65
 as Sack Knot, 98
 tying instructions, 100, 102–3
Cow Hitch (Lark's Head)
 Inside Cow Hitch, 92, 93–95
 Toggled Lark's Head, 145,
  147–48
 tying instructions, 92–93
 uses for, 48
Cross Knot (True Lover's Knot),
  61–63
Crown Knot See Wall and Crown
  Knot
Crown Sennit
 five-strand Sennit, 10, 130, 131
 six-strand Sennit, 140, 141
cutting rope, 17–19

Dacron rope, 11, 17
decorative knots. See knots, decorative
dimpling, 105
dock lines, 16, 25–26, 27–28
double-braid rope
 construction, 14–15
 Eye Splice, 118–22
Double Sheet Bend, 65, 68, 70, 71

dowels, 34
dyeing line, 20–22
Dyneema SK75 rope, 12, 17

ends of line. See line ends
Eye Splices, 10, 116–25, 145
 double-braid rope, 118–22
 end of laid rope, 70, 116–18, 149
 middle of laid rope, 122–25

fids, 30–32
Figure-Eight Knot, 10, 38, 40
Flemish Coil, 29, 30
forward loop, 7
fray prevention, 14, 18–19, 22–24

gathering hitch instructions,
  97–103
 Binder's Loop, 97–98
 Constrictor Knot, 98, 100, 102–3
 Sack Knot (Thrice-Turned), 98,
  100
 Sack Knot (Twice-Turned), 98,
  99
 Strangle Knot, 98–99, 101
gluing rope, 19–20

half hitch
 Anchor Bend and, 86
 Bowline and, 8
 Clove Hitches and, 8, 80, 82
 Cockscombing and, 143–45
 Constrictor Knot and, 8
 Round Turn with Two Half
  Hitches, 48, 78–80
 Tugboat (Bitt) Hitch and, 92
 tying instructions, 8
halyards, 16, 17
Hawser Bend, 74–76
heat, and joining rope, 19–20
heat-cutting rope, 17–19
Heaving Line Knot, 38, 42–44
hemostats, 32–33
hitches, 9, 10, 78
hitches, tying instructions for
 Anchor Bend, 82, 85–86
 attaching hitches, 78–97
 Binder's Loop, 97–98
 Bitt Hitch (Tugboat Hitch),
  91–92

155

Index

hitches, tying instructions for
(continued)
  Buntline Hitch, 88, 89
  Cleat Hitch, 82, 84
  Clove Hitch for short piles, 82, 83
  Clove Hitch for tall piles, 80–82
  Constrictor Knot, 98, 100, 102–3
  Cow Hitch (Lark's Head), 92–93
  gathering hitches, 78, 97–103
  Inside Cow Hitch, 92, 93–95
  Jar Sling, 95–97
  Jug Sling Knot, 95–97
  Lark's Head (Cow Hitch), 92–93
  Rolling Hitch, 86–88
  Round Turn with Two Half Hitches, 78–80
  Sack Knot (Thrice-Turned), 98, 100
  Sack Knot (Twice-Turned), 98, 99
  Slipped Buntline Hitch, 88, 90–91
  Strangle Knot, 98–99, 101
  Tugboat Hitch (Bitt Hitch), 91–92
hockle, 26, 27

Inside Cow Hitch, 92, 93–95

jam turn, 5–6
Japanese Bowline, 57–59
Japanese Success Knot, 7, 63–64
Jar Sling, 7, 10, 95–97
joining rope, 19–20
Jug Sling Knot, 95–97
Jury Mast Knot, 65–67

kebab skewer, 32
Kevlar rope, 12
kinked line, 26, 27
knife, rigging, 19, 30, 31
knots
  effect of, on line, 9
  history, 1–2
  instructions for, 10
  phases of tying, 10
  purpose of, 9–10
  tools for, 30–36
  tying or casting, 3

knots, decorative
  Bell Rope Sennit, 140–42
  Cockscombing, 143–45
  Crown Sennit, 130, 131
  joining, 19–20
  line ends, 126–45
  Star Knot, 132, 135–39
  Tack Knot, 130, 132, 133–34
  Toggle and Becket, 148–49
  Toggled Lark's Head, 145, 147–48
  Toggled Reef Knot, 145, 146
  toggle knots, 145–49
  Turk's Head, 126–29
knots, tying instructions for
  Angler's Loop (Perfection Knot), 50, 52–53
  Blood Knot, 41–42
  Bowline, 46, 47
  Bowline on a Bight, 46, 48–50
  Clover Knot (True Lover's Knot), 61–63
  Cross Knot (True Lover's Knot), 61–63
  Figure-Eight Knot, 38, 40
  Heaving Line Knot, 38, 42–44
  Japanese Bowline, 57–59
  Japanese Success Knot, 63–64
  Jury Mast Knot, 65–67
  loop knots, 46–67
  Monkey's Fist, 42, 44–46
  Overhand Knot, 37, 38
  Painter's Bowline, 50, 54
  Perfection Knot (Angler's Loop), 50, 52–53
  Slip Knot, 37–38, 39
  Slipped Bowline, 46, 50, 51
  Slipped Overhand Knot, 37–38, 39
  Spanish Bowline, 55–56
  Stevedore Knot, 38, 41
  stopper knots, 37–46
  Three-Part Crown Knot, 59–61
  True Lover's Knot (Clover Knot or Cross Knot), 61–63

laid rope
  construction, 13–14
  Eye Splice at end of, 70, 116–18, 149

Index

Eye Splice in middle of, 122–25
hockle, 26, 27
Lark's Head (Cow Hitch)
  Inside Cow Hitch, 92, 93–95
  Toggled Lark's Head, 145,
    147–48
  tying instructions, 92–93
  uses for, 48
lead weights, 35
line ends
  fray prevention, 14, 18–19,
    22–24
  knots, decorative, 126–45
  splices, 104–12
  stopper knots, 37–46
  whipping lines, 14, 22–24
line. *See also* rope
  basic configurations, 4–8
  breaking strength, 8, 13
  care of, 25–29
  dyeing, 20–22
  joining, 19–20
  knots, effect of, 9
  part (break), 8
  parts of, 3–4
  rope versus, 3–4
  seizing lines, 24–25
  selection according to use, 16–17
  storage, 29–30
  strength, 8–9, 11–13, 21, 22
  washing lines, 28–29
  whipping lines, 14, 22–24
  working strength, 8–9, 13
Long Splice, 10, 114–16
loop knot instructions, 46–67
  Angler's Loop (Perfection Knot),
    50, 52–53
  Bowline, 46, 47
  Bowline on a Bight, 46, 48–50
  Clover Knot (True Lover's Knot),
    61–63
  Cross Knot (True Lover's Knot),
    61–63
  Japanese Bowline, 57–59
  Japanese Success Knot, 63–64
  Jury Mast Knot, 65–67
  Painter's Bowline, 50, 54
  Perfection Knot (Angler's Loop),
    50, 52–53
  Slipped Bowline, 46, 50, 51

Spanish Bowline, 55–56
Three-Part Crown Knot, 59–61
True Lover's Knot (Clover Knot
  or Cross Knot), 61–63

marlinespike, definition of, 2
marlinespike seamanship, 2, 3–10
marlinespike seamanship tools,
  30–36
masking tape, 35
Matthew Walker Knot, 20
  Bell Rope Sennit, 140, 141–42
  line preparation, 17
  tying instructions, 110–12
  uses for, 105
measuring tape, 35
Monkey's Fist, 20
  tools for, 10, 30
  tying instructions, 44–46
  uses for, 42
  weights for, 35

needle, sailmaker's, 33
nylon rope, 11, 21, 22

Overhand Knot, 8, 37, 38
overhand loop, 7
ozone, protecting lines from, 27

painters, 17
Painter's Bowline, 50, 54
palm protection, 34
parallel-core rope, 15–16
part (break), 8
Perfection Knot (Angler's Loop), 7,
  8, 50, 52–53
polyester rope, 11
polyethylene rope, 11, 12
polypropylene rope, 11

Reef (Square) Knot
  seizing lines, 24
  Toggled Reef Knot, 145, 146
  tying instructions, 76–77
rigging knife, 19, 30, 31
Rolling Hitch, 86–88
rope. *See also* line
  characteristics, 3
  construction, 12, 13–16
  cutting, 17–19

157

Index

rope *(continued)*
  damage signs, 25
  fray prevention, 14, 18–19, 22–24
  history, 1–2
  line versus, 3–4
  materials, 11–12
  properties, 12–13
  selection according to use, 16–17
  strength, 8–9, 11–13, 21, 22
rope ends. *See* line ends
ropework, 2
round turn, 6–7
Round Turn with Two Half
  Hitches, 48, 78–80
rubber snubbers, 26

Sack Knot (Thrice-Turned), 98,
  100, 130, 132, 143
Sack Knot (Twice-Turned), 98, 99,
  113, 130, 143
sailmaker's needle, 33
sailmaker's palm, 34
sailor's knife, 19, 30, 31
seizing lines, 24–25
Sennits, 19, 130
  Bell Rope Sennit, 19, 140–42
  five-strand Crown Sennit, 10,
    130, 131
  six-strand Crown Sennit, 140,
    141
Sheet Bend, 4
  Double Sheet Bend, 65, 68, 70, 71
  effect of, on line, 9
  purpose of, 10
  tying instructions, 68–70
sheets, 4, 16
shock loading of line, 26
Short Splice
  instructions, 113–14
  purpose of, 10
  strength loss, 112
single-braid rope, 14, 15
Slip Knot, 37–38, 39
Slipped Bowline, 46, 50, 51
Slipped Buntline Hitch, 88, 90–91
Slipped Overhand Knot, 37–38, 39
small stuff, 23–24
Spanish Bowline, 55–56
Spectra 1000 rope, 12, 17
splices, 9, 10, 104

splices, types of
  Back Splice, 105, 106–7
  for connecting line, 112–16
  Eye Splice, double-braid rope,
    118–22
  Eye Splice, end of laid rope, 70,
    116–18
  Eye Splice, middle of laid rope,
    122–25
  for line ends, 104–12
  Long Splice, 114–16
  Matthew Walker Knot, 110–12
  Short Splice, 112, 113–14
  spliced eyes, 116–25
  Wall and Crown Knot, 105,
    108–9
spring clamps, 33
Square (Reef) Knot
  seizing lines, 24
  Toggled Reef Knot, 145, 146
  tying instructions, 76–77
Star Knot
  Bell Rope Sennit, 140, 142
  glue use, 19–20
  Sack Knot (Twice-Turned) and, 98
  tools for, 10, 32
  tying instructions, 132, 135–39
Stevedore Knot, 38, 41
stopper knot instructions, 37–46
  Blood Knot, 41–42
  Figure-Eight Knot, 38, 40
  Heaving Line Knot, 38, 42–44
  Monkey's Fist, 44–46
  Overhand Knot, 37, 38
  Slip Knot, 37–38, 39
  Slipped Overhand Knot, 37–38,
    39
  Stevedore Knot, 38, 41
storage of line, 29–30
Strangle Knot, 98–99, 101, 105
sunlight, protecting lines from, 27
surgical hemostats, 32–33

Tack Knot
  Bell Rope Sennit and, 140, 142
  Crown Sennit and, 130
  glue use, 19–20
  Sack Knot (Twice-Turned) and,
    98
  tools for, 10, 30

Index

tying instructions, 130, 132, 133–34
tape, masking, 35
Technora rope, 12, 17
thimbles, 26, 27
Three-Part Crown Knot, 59–61
Three-Strand Cockscomb. *See* Cockscombing
three-strand rope, 13–14
toggle, 35–36
Toggle and Becket, 148–49
Toggled Lark's Head, 145, 147–48
Toggled Reef Knot, 145, 146
toolbox, 35
towlines, 17
True Lover's Knot (Clover Knot or Cross Knot), 61–63
Tugboat Hitch (Bitt Hitch), 91–92
Turk's Head
  tools for, 32, 34
  tying instructions, 10, 126–29
turn, 5
  jam turn, 5–6
  round turn, 6–7

underhand loop, 7
U.S. Power Squadrons (USPS) website, 3

Vectran rope, 12, 17

Wall and Crown Knot, 20, 105, 108–9, 130, 132, 149
washing lines, 28–29
water rescue work, 46, 48
waterskiing lines, 17
whipping lines, 14, 22–24
working part, 4
working strength of line, 8–9, 13

159

United States Power Squadrons is all about boating education, safety, and enjoyment

United States Power Squadrons (USPS) is a private organization with 50,000 enthusiastic members interested in all types of boating—motoring, sailing, paddling, rowing, fishing, cruising, hunting, and water sports—in 450 squadrons in the United States, Puerto Rico, and Japan.

USPS is all about education and sharing boating experiences. Through our courses, books, guides, presentations, and seminars, we've been teaching safe boating since 1914. USPS members include experts from the boating world: authors of leading marine books, magazine articles, and guides; USCG licensed masters and captains; and participants of many boards and commissions on marine topics worldwide. USPS members and the public enjoy courses created and taught by our volunteer instructors, at very reasonable costs. Courses and seminars include:

- Basic Boating
- Seamanship
- GPS
- Coastal and Inland Navigation
- Understanding and Using Charts
- Offshore Navigation
- Celestial Navigation
- Marine Weather
- Marine Electronics
- Marine Engine Maintenance
- Cruise Planning
- Sailing
- Instructor Development and Certification

Members place a high value on fellowship through social events and civic service. Our members actively participate in the boating community through education, vessel safety checks, and a cooperative program with the National Oceanic and Atmospheric Administration (NOAA) to update navigation charts. USPS even maintains a network of port captains who provide expert local information for visiting boaters.

Perhaps the greatest benefit of participation with the United States Power Squadrons is the enjoyment, camaraderie, and opportunity to share experiences and ideas with other members, and to help the boating public. United States Power Squadrons endeavors to make boating a safer, more enjoyable experience for everyone. To learn more, visit www.usps.org.

Look for these other USPS Guides:

The Boatowner's Guide to GMDSS and Marine Radio
Celestial Sight Reduction Methods
Compass Installation and Adjusting
Marine Amateur Radio
Radar and GPS